ASTRID BROWN

The Healing Herbal Teas

Everything on How to Brew, Enjoy, & Benefit from Therapeutic Brews

Featuring 100+ Recipes for Stronger Immunity & Lifelong Vitality

ALL IN 1

Table of Contents

Introduction

Herbal teas have been natural remedies for centuries, deeply rooted in the traditions of our ancestors. Yet, in the rush of modern life and the shadow of contemporary medicine, they have been pushed aside and forgotten as a simple yet powerful wellness practice.

Distilled from years of exploration, this book aims to bridge that gap, reconnecting you with the healing power of herbal teas. Through these pages, you will discover techniques, tips, and strategies to incorporate herbal teas into your daily routine, embracing a more natural and balanced approach to health.

The benefits you will discover here are as varied as the herbs themselves. From the calming embrace of a chamomile infusion to the vibrant zing of a ginger decoction, herbal teas offer a spectrum of wellness benefits. Each chapter unfurls these benefits like leaves in hot water, revealing their essence through practical knowledge, recipes, and rituals.

With this book, allow yourself to journey back to basics, where you learn to appreciate the simplicity and effectiveness of nature's gifts.

Chapter 1

History of Herbal Teas

Herbal teas have long been valued for their soothing flavors, purported health benefits, and deep roots in culture and tradition. As you delve into this chapter, you will learn about the ancient origins of herbal tea in civilizations like China, Egypt, and Greece, where these nature-infused brews were deeply intertwined with spirituality, ceremony, and healing practices. Tracing the winding paths of trade routes, you will discover how herbal tea traditions spread across borders. The impacts of these botanical brews will unfold, from their significance in culture to their role in traditional remedies.

Herbal Tea Through the Years

Herbal tea, a concoction brewed from various plants, herbs, and spices, has been a part of human civilization for thousands of years.

Origin in Ancient Civilizations

The tradition of brewing leaves, flowers, and other botanical elements into comforting beverages is as old as civilization. If you venture back into the annals of history, you will find that the ancient civilizations of China, Egypt, and Greece were the early trailblazers in herbal teas. Each of these ancient societies discovered herbal teas for the taste and wellness they imparted.

China

In ancient China, the discovery of tea is a tale steeped in legend, tracing back to Emperor Shen Nong in 2737 BC, when the first leaves were said to have fluttered into his boiling water, revealing not just a drink but an elixir for the soul. The Chinese deeply revered tea, understanding its potential to heal and rejuvenate, which led to the intricate art of the tea ceremony, known as Gongfu Cha. Far beyond simple brewing, this ritual is a testament to the esteem held for the humble tea leaf, turning its preparation into a dance of precision and respect.

Gongfu Cha is a masterful display of dedication. Each movement in the ceremony is deliberate, and each step, from leaf selection to pouring, is performed with grace and attentiveness. The ceremony is less about the tea itself and more about the experience, promoting a meditative state of mindfulness cherished over the centuries. In honoring the tea, you also honor the lineage of skilled hands that have nurtured and crafted it from garden to cup, recognizing tea's journey through history.

Sipping tea during Gongfu Cha is an invitation to savor life's simplicity and quieter moments, fully engaging with the array of subtle flavors and aromas that each pours over the leaves unfurls. It is a celebration not just of a beverage but of culture, tranquility, and the joy found in the smallest of acts—a rich Chinese tradition that elevates the daily ritual of drinking tea to a meaningful, almost spiritual act.

Egypt

The ancient Egyptians were not only architectural pioneers but also forerunners in the sophisticated use of herbal infusions, which they integrated deeply into their health and spiritual practices. The reverence they held for the natural world is vividly captured in the remnants of their papyrus scrolls, such as the renowned Ebers Papyrus, dating back to 1550 BC. This ancient medical document provides a window into the Egyptians' herbal knowledge, featuring over 700 remedies and magical formulas. Every brew was crafted with intention, harnessing ingredients like mint, anise, and chamomile, which they believed to possess potent healing properties.

These herbal teas served multiple purposes, from medicinal treatments to important roles in religious ceremonies, and were thought to be favored by the gods themselves. Egyptians understood the natural herbs to be gifts from the deities, and as such, the brewing and consumption of these teas were conducted with great respect and care. For instance, mint was savored for its refreshing taste and purported digestive benefits, while anise was often employed to help soothe and promote sleep. The methods of steeping and combining these herbs were meticulous, evolving over centuries into a deeply rooted cultural practice that echoed their connection to the land and their devotion to wellness.

Herbal infusions were also entwined with the Egyptians' practices surrounding preserving the body in life and preparing for the afterlife. Ingredients commonly used in teas were simultaneously used in the embalming process, speaking to their significant antimicrobial properties and the Egyptians' advanced understanding of herbal benefits. Beyond their physical health benefits, these herbal concoctions were believed to purify the spirit, enhance concentration during meditative practices, and even serve as offerings to the gods, interweaving the practical, the sacred, and the ceremonial into a holistic approach to life and death.

Greece and Europe

Long ago in ancient Greece, people like Hippocrates and Dioscorides were fascinated by the healing powers of herbs and wrote about them. For them, drinking herbal tea is a way to health and comfort, exploring its benefits with a scientific eye. This curiosity helped lay the foundation for herbal remedies and practices that spread across Europe.

In medieval Europe, especially among the mystics in Celtic areas, the tradition of reading tea leaves, known as tasseography, took root. Although it is unknown exactly where or how this practice started, it became a cherished part of European tea culture, showing their love for mysterious and hidden meanings.

Tasseography, or tea leaf reading, is an ancient practice with unclear origins. It reflects the natural urge to seek answers in nature. The Celts, known for their mystical traditions, might have helped develop this art. In tasseography, each tea leaf in the cup becomes a symbol to interpret. Readers investigate the cup as if it is a gateway, finding meaning and predictions in the patterns of the wet leaves.

Thus, herbal tea and tasseography are two different but connected traditions from the ancient world. Based on the knowledge of early doctors and healers, herbal tea was used for physical and spiritual health. Tasseography was used to explore destiny and uncover hidden messages. Together, these practices show how people in the past respected the benefits of herbal teas and the mysterious messages they could hold.

Different ancient civilizations had their ways of using herbal teas. The Chinese were known for their detailed classification of herbs and brewing skills. The Egyptians combined their use of herbal teas with their religious beliefs. The Greeks, on the other hand, were interested in the scientific aspects of herbal teas and laid the groundwork for herbal medicine.

Religious and Ceremonial Use

Steeped in warm waters and rich traditions, the essence of herbal tea transcends the simplistic act of quenching thirst. It connects us to ancient cultures where making and drinking tea was a sacred practice, a way to feel closer to ancestors and the divine.

In Asia, for example, the quiet rituals of tea ceremonies in Buddhist monasteries are about mindfulness and peace. Every step, from boiling water to sipping tea, helps to connect the drinker's mind and body with the universe.

Across the globe in North America, Native American tribes see herbal tea as a way to communicate with nature. For them, the herbs in their tea carry messages from the natural world, making brewing and drinking tea a sacred act of seeking wisdom and giving thanks, often accompanied by drumming and chanting.

Herbal tea also brings people together, creating a sense of community. Sharing a cup can strengthen friendships, mark important moments, and offer comfort during tough times. This communal aspect of tea drinking is valued in cultures all around the world.

Using herbal teas in religious and ceremonial settings shows how simple natural elements can have deep spiritual and social significance. A simple cup of tea can bridge the earthly and divine gap, connecting you to the larger world. Through the steam of a hot cup of tea, you can find ancient wisdom, a sense of community, and a touch of something beyond yourself, carrying on traditions that have been cherished for generations.

Impact of Trade Routes

The annals of history vividly sketch the bustling scenes of ancient trade routes, where the clatter of camel hooves on the Silk Road and the rustle of sails in maritime routes narrated tales of adventure, commerce, and cultural exchange. Along these veins of trade, the seeds of herbal tea traditions were carried from one region to another, blossoming into a global phenomenon that transcends geographical and cultural boundaries.

As traders, laden with an assortment of goods, traversed across continents, they carried with them the whispers of their homeland, encapsulated within the delicate leaves, flowers, and seeds destined to be brewed into herbal teas. The Silk Road, a historic nexus of trade between the East and West, was not merely a conduit for silk, spices, and other goods but a passage through which the tradition of herbal teas flowed.

Traders from China introduced the calming brews of chamomile and peony to the bustling bazaars of Persia and the Middle East. In return, they carried back with them the exotic flavors of Persian mint and Arabian jasmine. Each interchange was a note in the symphony of cultural amalgamation that enriched the global tapestry of herbal tea traditions.

The maritime trade routes, the veins of commerce across the seas, were further responsible for the flow of herbal tea traditions. As ships harbored in distant lands, the chests of herbs and teas were unloaded onto foreign soils, each grain a potential seed for new traditions. The shores of Europe, Africa, and the distant islands in the Pacific witnessed the dawn of herbal tea traditions through the hands of traders who sailed across oceans.

The impact of trade routes on the evolution of herbal tea traditions is a tale of humanity's innate curiosity and the boundless quest for exploration. It is a narrative where every exchange was a step towards a global community, where the essence of diverse cultures was shared, celebrated, and blended into a common legacy.

Health Benefits

Herbal teas have long been a comfort and tradition, offering health benefits such as:

Digestive Aid

Herbal teas could support the digestive system. Peppermint tea, for example, is known for its antispasmodic properties, which can help relieve symptoms of irritable bowel syndrome (IBS) and other digestive disorders. Similarly, ginger tea helps ease nausea and combat bloating and gas, making it a favored choice after a heavy meal.

Sleep and Relaxation

In a world where stress is a common adversary, herbal teas like chamomile and lavender serve as gentle allies, promoting relaxation and aiding sleep. Chamomile tea, known for its mild sedative properties, has been a popular choice for those looking to improve their sleep quality. Lavender tea, with its soothing aroma, also provides a tranquil escape, reducing stress and promoting sleep.

Immune Boost

In traditional medicine, herbal teas have been lauded for the potential to bolster the immune system. Echinacea tea is often reached for at the onset of a cold and is believed to help bolster the body's defense against common illnesses. Likewise, teas made from herbs like elderberry and ginseng have been associated with immune-boosting properties, providing natural support against seasonal ailments.

Heart Health

Certain herbal teas also come with the promise of supporting heart health. Hibiscus tea, for instance, has been linked to lower blood pressure levels, which is a significant factor in promoting heart health. Green tea, rich in antioxidants, has also been associated with various heart-healthy benefits, including improved cholesterol levels.

Metabolic Support

Green tea is rich in catechins linked to burning fat and boosting metabolism. Many people who want to lose weight or stay in shape choose green tea.

Cultural Significance

Brewing and sharing herbal teas are often linked to rituals, hospitality, and a sense of community in different cultures.

Symbol of Hospitality and Communal Bonds

Herbal teas have historically been a symbol of hospitality. Brewing a pot of tea for guests is a universal gesture of welcome. It creates an environment conducive to conversations, sharing, and forming or strengthening communal bonds. In many cultures, offering a cup of herbal tea is synonymous with extending friendship, respect, and camaraderie. It is a humble gesture transcending linguistic or cultural barriers, embodying a universal language of warmth and hospitality.

Rituals and Traditions

The brewing and consumption of herbal teas are often encompassed in rituals that reflect a community's values, aesthetics, and mindfulness. These rituals add a layer of significance to the act of drinking tea. They provide a structured space for reflection, appreciation, and adherence to traditional practices passed down through generations. Through these rituals, herbal teas become a vessel for preserving and celebrating cultural heritage.

Mindfulness and Tranquility

Brewing and sipping herbal tea is a calming ritual. It starts with water heating, then the quiet steam from a hot cup, and the soothing warmth as you drink slowly. This process is a peaceful break in a busy day. It helps you focus on the now, enjoying the smell and taste of the tea and maybe even the people you are with.

Expressions of Cultural Identity

Different herbs and brewing practices often reflect diverse geographies and cultural identities. Herbal teas become a means through which individuals express, share, and celebrate their cultural heritage. They carry stories of ancestral wisdom, traditional medicine, and the rich biodiversity of the regions they originate from. Each blend of herbal tea is a narrative, offering a taste of the land, the climate, and the cultural ethos from where it springs.

Folk Remedies

Exploring herbal teas means learning about traditional folk remedies. These are simple, time-tested health solutions passed down through generations.

Understanding Folk Remedies

Folk remedies are traditional health solutions passed down through generations, often based on local natural resources. Herbal teas are a common folk remedy, offering a simple, natural way to support health and well-being.

Learning about folk remedies opens the door to understanding the traditional wisdom behind herbal teas. It helps you appreciate the potential benefits of different herbs and deepens your connection to the cultural heritage each cup represents.

Knowing about folk remedies also guides you in exploring which herbal teas might suit your health goals or personal tastes. However, approach this knowledge with an open mind and caution, respecting the limits of traditional wisdom and considering modern scientific evidence and medical advice for serious health issues.

Global Glimpses of Herbal Teas as Folk Remedies

In Europe, people brew elderberry tea to fight colds and flu, showing their trust in nature's healing powers. In South America, the energizing Yerba Mate tea is popular for its vitality-boosting effects.

Different regions have favorite herbs for making teas to address common health issues. For example, chamomile tea is known for its calming effects and is often used for better sleep and relaxation. In East Asia, ginseng tea is valued for its ability to refresh the body and mind.

The tradition of using herbal teas as folk remedies connects the past with the present. It encourages people to explore the rich history of natural wellness, learn from the experiences of past generations, and continue the tradition of holistic well-being.

Chapter 2

Healing Herbs Around the World

This captivating chapter unveils the ancient traditions, rituals, and secrets of teas that have nurtured health and wellness across continents for centuries. Discover the harmonizing power of Traditional Chinese Medicine teas, the mindfulness imbued in Japanese Matcha, and the holistic wellness of Indian Ayurvedic brews.

Travel to Africa to savor the rich flavors of Rooibos and Honeybush, experience the refreshing hospitality of Moroccan Mint Tea, and explore the ancient herbal wisdom of Ethiopia. Then, dive into the lush Amazonian rainforest for a sip of its life-affirming brews and join South America's communal Mate circles, where sharing a drink is sharing life.

Each section of this chapter is a gateway to the diverse and vibrant world of herbal healing, offering not just recipes but a taste of the cultural significance and communal spirit that these teas embody. From the highlands of China to the heart of the Amazon, it is an invitation to experience the unity of humanity through the shared tradition of herbal teas. Get ready to awaken your senses, soothe your soul, and discover the healing power of nature's finest herbs.

Asian Healing Teas

In Asia, tea is more than a mere drink; it's a ritual, a form of medicine, and a way of life. The philosophy surrounding tea is that it harmonizes the body, mind, and spirit, creating a sense of equilibrium. From the verdant tea gardens of Japan to the highlands of China and the spice-laden air of India, each region offers its unique blend of healing teas, each with its own story.

Traditional Chinese Medicine Teas

At the heart of Traditional Chinese Medicine (TCM), teas are not just beverages; they are potent medicinal concoctions designed to harmonize the body's Qi (vital energy), balance the Yin and Yang, and enhance the functions of different organs. TCM teas are a rich tapestry of herbs, roots, flowers, and leaves, each selected for its specific healing properties, guided by millennia of wisdom and practice. These teas are tailored to individual needs, aiming to prevent and treat diseases by addressing their root causes.

Here are some of the most cherished teas in TCM and their preparation methods.

Green Tea

Green tea, whose origins are traced back to China, is celebrated not only for its rich cultural significance but also for its profound health benefits. Its high concentration of catechins, potent antioxidants, positions green tea as a powerful defender against oxidative stress, inflammation, and chronic diseases. Regular consumption is linked to a myriad of health benefits, including enhanced cardiovascular health, improved brain function, and a reduced risk of certain types of cancer.

Classic Chinese Green Tea Recipe

In Chinese culture, preparing green tea is an art form that respects the delicate nature of the tea leaves. The key is to use water that's about to boil (around 80-85°C or 176-185°F), as too hot water can make the tea taste bitter. Use about 2 grams of tea leaves for every 6 ounces of water. This method ensures the preservation of the tea's delicate flavors and health-promoting properties. Here's a simple recipe you can follow:

Ingredients:

- 2 grams of green tea leaves
- 6 ounces of hot water (80-85°C or 176-185°F)
- Optional: A few jasmine flowers for a floral scent

Instructions:
Steep the green tea leaves (and jasmine flowers, if using) in hot water for 2-3 minutes. Strain and enjoy the tea's natural, subtle flavors and aroma.

Chrysanthemum Tea

Chrysanthemum tea is another vital component of TCM known for its cooling properties. It is often recommended for its ability to reduce heat and inflammation in the body, making it perfect for soothing sore throats, reducing fever, and enhancing eye health.

Refreshing Chrysanthemum Tea Recipe

This recipe combines dried chrysanthemum flowers steeped in hot water with optional goji berries and honey for extra flavor and health benefits. This creates a refreshingly floral and slightly sweet beverage that can be enjoyed hot or cold.

Ingredients:

- A handful of dried chrysanthemum flowers
- Hot water
- Goji berries for added flavor and health benefits; honey to sweeten

Instructions:
Steep the chrysanthemum flowers (and goji berries, if using) in hot water for 5 minutes. Strain and sweeten with honey if desired. This tea is especially refreshing when served cold, offering a floral and slightly sweet taste.

Goji Berry Tea

Goji berries are vibrant red fruits rich in antioxidants. They are commonly brewed into a nourishing tea, which is celebrated for its vision-protecting zeaxanthin content, immune-boosting vitamin C, and overall skin health benefits.

Nutrient-Rich Goji Berry Infusion Recipe

This Goji Berry Tea recipe is simple yet potent. The sweetness and health benefits of goji berries create a soothing and nutritious drink that is perfect for any time of the day. For additional taste, blend it with red dates or honey.

Ingredients:

- 1 tablespoon of dried goji berries
- 8 ounces of hot water
- Optional: Red dates or honey for sweetness

Instructions:
Steep the goji berries in hot water for about 10 minutes. The berries will plump up, releasing their flavors and nutrients into the

water. For additional sweetness and health benefits, add red dates or a spoonful of honey.

Japanese Matcha

Unlike regular green tea, which involves steeping whole leaves in water, matcha is a fine, vibrant green powder made from shade-grown tea leaves, offering a richer concentration of antioxidants, chlorophyll, and amino acids, particularly L-Theanine. This composition contributes to matcha's ability to promote relaxation without drowsiness, alongside enhancing alertness and concentration. Matcha's preparation and consumption are deeply rooted in Zen Buddhism, reflecting the practice of mindfulness and the art of living in the moment. It is renowned for its ability to enhance calm, boost concentration, and provide a sustained energy release, making it a favorite among tea connoisseurs and health enthusiasts alike.

Classic Ceremonial Matcha Recipe

Master the art of preparing matcha in the traditional Japanese way with this recipe. This promises a tea experience that's as rich in flavor as it is in heritage, offering a tranquil moment to savor the vibrant essence of matcha and its myriad health benefits.

Ingredients:

- 1-2 teaspoons of matcha powder
- 2 ounces of hot water (just under boiling)
- Bamboo whisk (chasen) for frothing

Instructions:
Sift the matcha powder into a bowl to remove any clumps. Add hot water and use the bamboo whisk to whisk vigorously in a "W" motion until frothy. Enjoy immediately to experience the full depth of its flavors and health benefits. This traditional method

celebrates the simplicity and elegance of Japanese tea culture, inviting a moment of peace and reflection in every sip.

Indian Ayurvedic Brews

Indian Ayurvedic Brews are steeped in a tradition that dates back thousands of years, focusing on balancing the body's doshas (vital energies): Vata, Pitta, and Kapha. These brews are more than just tea; they are a blend of herbs, spices, and plants that are used to promote health, vitality, and balance within the body and mind. Ayurvedic teas often include ingredients like turmeric, ginger, basil (Tulsi), cardamom, and cinnamon, each chosen for its specific healing properties and ability to support different bodily functions.

One of the most celebrated Ayurvedic teas is Tulsi Tea, revered as "The Queen of Herbs" for its powerful adaptogenic properties. It helps in reducing stress, bolstering the immune system, and balancing the body's energy levels. Another staple is Turmeric Tea, known for its anti-inflammatory and antioxidant benefits, which can aid in digestion, immune function, and pain relief.

Tulsi Ginger Tea Recipe

This recipe combines the soothing qualities of Tulsi leaves with the warm zest of fresh ginger, steeped together to create a comforting tea that's perfect for enhancing digestion and vitality. Honey adds a touch of sweetness to this healing brew.

Ingredients:

- 1 teaspoon of dried Tulsi leaves
- ½ inch of fresh ginger, grated
- 1 cup of boiling water
- Honey (optional, for sweetness)

Instructions:
Steep the Tulsi leaves and grated ginger in boiling water for 5-7 minutes. Strain the mixture into a cup and add honey to taste if desired. This tea is perfect for soothing the nerves, improving digestion, and enhancing overall vitality.

African Herbal Potions

In the heart of the vast and vibrant continent of Africa lies a rich tapestry of flora that has nourished and healed communities for centuries. I invite you on a journey through the diverse landscapes of Africa to discover the ancient and modern uses of its most cherished plants. You'll start with the serene valleys of South Africa, home to the globally beloved Rooibos and Honeybush, herbs renowned for their delicious, healthful teas that soothe the body and spirit. Then, traverse the bustling markets and serene landscapes of Morocco, where the ritual of Moroccan Mint Tea signifies hospitality and friendship, offering a refreshing blend that captivates the senses. Your exploration takes you further to the highlands of Ethiopia, where unique Herbal Mixes reveal the intricate balance of flavors and benefits, steeped in traditions that predate the written word.

Rooibos and Honeybush

Diving into the heart of African herbal traditions, Rooibos and Honeybush emerge as two remarkable herbal teas, each with its unique flavor profile and health benefits. These teas, native to South Africa, have been celebrated for centuries for their healing properties and are now gaining popularity worldwide for their wellness contributions.

Rooibos, also known as Red Bush, and Honeybush are cousins in the plant world. Each thrives in South Africa's unique climate and soil conditions. Rooibos is distinguished by its vibrant red color and slightly sweet, earthy taste, while Honeybush is named for its honey-scented flowers, offering a sweeter and lighter flavor profile.

Rooibos is caffeine-free, making it an excellent choice for people of all ages, including those who are sensitive to caffeine. It is rich in antioxidants, such as aspalathin and nothofagin, which help combat free radicals in the body, reducing the risk of chronic diseases. Rooibos is also known for its calming effects, aiding in sleep and stress relief.

Honeybush shares similar health benefits, including antioxidant properties, but is particularly noted for its potential to support respiratory health due to its pinitol content, which can help soothe coughs.

Rooibos Tea Recipe

This traditional brew highlights the smooth, naturally sweet flavor of Rooibos leaves.

Ingredients:

- 1 teaspoon of Rooibos leaves
- 8 ounces of boiling water

Instructions:
Steep Rooibos leaves in boiling water for 5-7 minutes. Enjoy as is, or add milk and honey for a richer taste.

Honeybush Iced Tea Recipe

Refreshing and aromatic, this Honeybush Iced Tea recipe is a summertime must-have.

Ingredients:

- 1 tablespoon of Honeybush leaves
- 8 ounces of boiling water
- Ice cubes
- Lemon slices and honey to taste

Instructions:
Brew Honeybush leaves in boiling water for 7-10 minutes. Cool and serve over ice with lemon slices and honey.

Moroccan Mint Tea

Moroccan Mint Tea, also known as Maghrebi mint tea, is a refreshing experience that transports you to the heart of Moroccan culture. Its preparation and consumption are acts of mindfulness, bringing people together and creating moments of peace and hospitality. Whether enjoyed in the bustling souks of Marrakech or the comfort of your home, Moroccan mint tea offers a taste of Morocco's rich heritage and the warmth of its people.

It plays a pivotal role in social interactions, serving as a gesture of welcome and a sign of friendship. It is traditionally served to guests, and refusing it is considered impolite, highlighting the tea's deep roots in Moroccan etiquette and hospitality. This tea, embodying the spirit of community, generosity, and tradition, is a testament to the timeless appeal of herbal teas around the world.

At the heart of this tea is the ritualistic manner in which it is prepared and served, often involving a ceremonial pouring from a height to create a frothy top, symbolizing the tea's quality and the host's skill.

Rich in antioxidants from the green tea base and the digestive aid from the mint, Moroccan mint tea is not only delightful but also beneficial for health. It aids in digestion, relieves stress, and can improve energy levels, making it a perfect choice for any time of the day.

Moroccan Mint Tea Recipe

Moroccan mint tea is a beverage that symbolizes friendship, hospitality, and social connection. Its vibrant green hue and invigorating aroma captivate the senses, making it a delightful accompaniment to lively conversations or serene moments of relaxation. Whether enjoyed in bustling marketplaces, intimate homes, or luxurious riads, Moroccan mint tea embodies the warmth and hospitality of Moroccan culture, inviting all who partake to savor its exquisite taste and the cherished traditions it represents. Here's a recipe to make one yourself.

Ingredients:

- 1 tablespoon loose green tea leaves
- A large handful of fresh mint leaves, washed
- 1/2 to 1 cup of sugar, depending on taste
- 4 cups of boiling water

Instructions:
In a teapot, combine the green tea leaves with a small amount of boiling water to rinse them, then drain. Add the mint leaves and sugar to the pot, fill it with the rest of the boiling water, and let it steep for about 5 minutes. Serve the tea in small glasses, pouring it from a height to create foam.

Ethiopian Herbal Tradition

Ethiopia, a land steeped in history and rich cultural traditions, offers a unique tapestry of herbal practices passed down through generations. Ethiopian herbal mixes are both a testament to the country's lush biodiversity and their deep-rooted belief in the healing powers of nature. These herbal concoctions are a cornerstone of Ethiopian traditional medicine, addressing a wide range of ailments from the common cold to more complex health issues.

In Ethiopia, the knowledge of herbs and their medicinal properties is a way of life. Families and traditional healers, known as "debteras," possess centuries-old wisdom, blending various herbs to create remedies that soothe, heal, and revitalize. Ethiopian herbal mixes are a vibrant fusion of Africa's botanical wealth, showcasing ingredients that are often unique to the region.

Key Ethiopian Herbs

Dive into the heart of Ethiopia's rich botanical heritage with these key herbs, each renowned for their unique healing properties.

- **Tenadam (Ruta chalepensis)**: Widely used for its analgesic and anti-inflammatory properties, Tenadam is a go-to herb for pain relief and soothing headaches.
- **Koseret (Lippia adoensis)**: This fragrant herb is cherished for its digestive and calming effects, often used in traditional Ethiopian cooking as well.
- **Tikur Azmud (Nigella sativa)**: Known globally as black seed, Tikur Azmud is celebrated for its immune-boosting properties.

Brewing Ethiopian Herbal Teas

Ethiopian herbal teas are a delightful way to experience the country's rich botanical heritage. Here's a simple recipe to get you started:

Ingredients:

- 1 teaspoon of dried Tenadam leaves
- 1 teaspoon of crushed Koseret leaves
- ½ teaspoon of Tikur Azmud (black seeds)
- Honey or sugar to taste
- 4 cups of boiling water

Instructions:
Combine the herbs in a teapot and pour boiling water over them. Allow the mixture to steep for 5-10 minutes, then strain. Sweeten with honey or sugar as desired. This tea offers a unique taste of Ethiopia's herbal tradition, providing a soothing and healthful experience.

South American Herbal Remedies

Embark on a verdant journey through the heart of South America, a continent teeming with ancient wisdom and natural remedies passed down through generations. Here you'll see rich traditions and vibrant cultures that harness the power of local flora for healing and harmony. Begin your exploration in the lush Amazon rainforest where the dense canopy hides a plethora of plants whose brews offer both healing and spiritual awakening. Venture further to the social gatherings of the Southern Cone, where mate culture thrives, uniting people over a shared gourd of this energizing and communal herbal drink. Ascend the majestic Andes in to uncover the high-altitude herbs and plants integral to indigenous medicine, offering resilience and health in the face of harsh climates.

Amazonian Brews

Amazonian herbal teas are as diverse as the rainforest itself, with each brew holding its unique story and benefits. These teas are made from the leaves, bark, roots, and flowers of plants that thrive in the rich, fertile soil of the Amazon. The indigenous peoples of the region have long harnessed these plants' therapeutic properties, using them to treat a wide range of ailments — from the common cold to more serious health conditions.

What sets these brews apart is their holistic approach to wellbeing. In addition to curing diseases, they also maintain balance within the body and mind, which fosters a deep sense of wellbeing. This holistic perspective mirrors the indigenous view of health, which sees the individual as an integral part of the larger ecosystem.

One of the most revered teas in the Amazon is made from the leaves of the Guayusa plant. Guayusa is prized for its smooth, slightly sweet flavor and energizing effects. Unlike the jittery buzz associated with coffee, Guayusa provides a unique kind of energy that is both uplifting and grounding. It is often consumed in the early hours of the morning, serving as a ceremonial way to start the day, connect with the spirits of the forest, and prepare for the challenges ahead.

Another beloved Amazonian brew is Cat's Claw tea, made from the bark of a vine believed to have powerful immune-boosting and anti-inflammatory properties. This tea has a rich history of use among indigenous tribes to ward off infections and promote overall health and vitality.

Amazonian Brews Recipes

Explore Amazon's vibrant heart through these recipes.

Guayusa Tea Recipe

To experience the gentle, sustained energy boost of Guayusa, follow this recipe:

Ingredients:

- 1 tablespoon of loose Guayusa leaves
- 1 cup of boiling water

Instructions:
Steep the Guayusa leaves in boiling water for 5 to 7 minutes, depending on your preferred strength. The result is a smooth,

mildly sweet tea that can be enjoyed at any time of the day to enhance focus, energy, and connection to the natural world.

Cat's Claw Tea Recipe

This recipe makes a soothing cup of Cat's Claw tea, known for its healing properties.

Ingredients:

- 1 teaspoon of Cat's Claw bark
- 1 cup of boiling water

Instructions:
Place the Cat's Claw bark in boiling water and let it simmer for about 15-20 minutes. Strain the tea and enjoy it warm. This brew is especially beneficial during the cold and flu season or whenever your immune system needs a boost.

Mate Culture

In the heart of South America, particularly in countries like Argentina, Uruguay, Paraguay, and southern Brazil, lies a cultural tradition that transcends mere beverage consumption. Mate (pronounced MAH-te), a traditional herbal tea, is not just a drink; it is a symbol of unity, friendship, and ritual, deeply embedded in these societies' social fabric.

Mate is made from the dried leaves of *Ilex paraguariensis, a* native South American plant. Its use predates European colonization, originating with the indigenous Guaraní people. For centuries, mate has been a communal experience, a form of social currency that fosters connection and conversation.

Central to mate culture is the concept of sharing. A single gourd (the traditional vessel for mate, often made from a hollowed-out calabash) and bombilla (a metal straw with a filter) are passed around in a group, symbolizing trust and community. The act of sharing a mate circle breaks down barriers, encouraging camaraderie and open dialogue.

The preparation and consumption of mate follow a set of rituals that vary slightly by region but always emphasize mindfulness and respect. The ceremonial aspect of mate drinking is a dance of tradition and etiquette, where the role of the *cebador* (the server) is important. This person is responsible for preparing the mate and managing its distribution among the participants, ensuring the mate is neither too strong nor too weak, maintaining the perfect balance of flavor.

To partake in this ritual is to understand the unwritten rules that govern it: not to stir the mate with the bombilla, to wait one's turn to drink, and to say "thank you" only when one has had enough and is stepping out of the circle. These rules ensure the smooth flow of the ceremony and deepen the sense of belonging and community among the participants.

Beyond its cultural significance, mate is revered for its health benefits. Rich in antioxidants, mate surpasses even green tea in its capacity to combat oxidative stress. It is also a source of vitamins and minerals, including vitamin C, B vitamins, and magnesium, contributing to bone health, cardiovascular health, and boosting the immune system. Furthermore, mate contains compounds that can aid in digestion and weight loss, making it a beloved choice for those seeking a natural boost to their health regimen.

Traditional Mate Recipe

Enjoying mate in this traditional manner allows one to savor the taste and engage in a ritual that has been passed down through generations, creating a bridge between the past and the present.

Ingredients:

- Yerba Mate: Approximately 50 grams (about 1/3 of the mate gourd)
- Hot water (not boiling): Approximately 70°C (158°F)
- A mate gourd
- A bombilla (metal straw)

Instructions:

1. Fill the mate gourd with yerba mate up to two-thirds.
2. Cover the gourd's mouth with your hand, invert it, and shake gently. This step helps the finer particles to settle on top, reducing the chance of clogging the bombilla.
3. Tilt the gourd to one side, creating a slope of yerba mate leaves. Slowly pour hot water into the lower (empty) part of the gourd.
4. Insert the bombilla into the wet side of the gourd, at the bottom.
5. Gently pour hot water into the gourd again, avoiding the dry side, to maintain flavor through multiple refills.

Andean Herbal Secrets

Nestled within the heart of South America, the Andes mountains are not only a spectacle of natural beauty but also a repository of ancient herbal wisdom. This region, rich in culture and biodiversity, harbors secrets of medicinal plants used by indigenous peoples for centuries. The Andean herbal secrets offer more than healing since they are also a gateway to understanding the intimate relationship between nature and human health embedded in the practices and traditions of local communities.

The Andes' unique ecosystem, characterized by high altitudes, diverse climates, and rich soils, cultivates some of the world's most potent medicinal plants. These herbs have adapted to harsh conditions, developing strong bioactive compounds. Communities across the Andes have, over millennia, discovered and harnessed these plants' properties, using them to treat a wide array of ailments in a holistic manner that respects the balance of body and mind.

Among the myriad of plants, a few stand out for their widespread use and significant health benefits. The *Muña*, known for its digestive and respiratory benefits, is revered for soothing stomach aches and combating altitude sickness. Meanwhile, *Valeriana* relaxes the nervous system, promoting sleep and reducing anxiety. The *Maca* root, often referred to as Andean ginseng, is lauded for its energy-boosting and hormonal balancing effects. Each plant carries stories of ancient wisdom passed down through generations, embodying the Andean spirit of harmony with nature.

Muña Tea Recipe

To bring a piece of the Andean magic into your home, here is a simple herbal tea recipesthat encapsulate the essence of Andean herbal traditions:

Ingredients:

- 1 tablespoon of dried Muña leaves
- 1 cup of boiling water

Instructions:

Steep the Muña leaves in boiling water for about 10 minutes. This minty, refreshing tea can be enjoyed after meals to aid digestion or during cold seasons to clear respiratory passages.

Chapter 3

Everything About Herbs

Herbs have been used for flavor, nutrition, and health for thousands of years. This chapter introduces different herb families, their unique flavors, uses, and health benefits. Learn about the classification system of herbs, which helps understand how different herbs are related. Explore also the distinct tastes of each family and some of their well-known members.

Herbal Families

Herbs have been used for centuries in cooking, medicine, and as ornamental plants. Knowing the different types of herbs and how they are categorized can help you better understand their unique properties and uses.

Mint Family

The Lamiaceae family, often called the mint family, is a treasure trove of aromatic, flavorful, and visually appealing herbs that have graced kitchen shelves and garden beds for centuries. Mint family played a role in traditional medicine and modern pharmaceuticals for its rich biochemical profile.

Characteristics

Understanding why certain herbs are grouped into this family requires a peek into their shared characteristics. The Lamiaceae family typically exhibits a square stem and opposite leaves, a unique trait. Often in whorls, their flowers are bilaterally symmetric, which means if you draw a line down the middle, each half is a mirror image of the other. The beautiful and diverse color palette of the flowers is another hallmark of this family, ranging from the soothing lavender to the vibrant pink and the serene white.

Taxonomy of Herbs

The Lamiaceae family, part of the Lamiales order, includes about 236 groups and over 7,000 types of plants. The diversity within this family is awe-inspiring, with species varying greatly in size, form, and function. However, despite this diversity, the shared characteristics like the square stems and aromatic properties create a common thread that binds them together.

Flavor Profiles

When it comes to taste, the Lamiaceae family offers a wide range. Many of these plants have a minty and sometimes sweet flavor, which makes them popular for cooking and making tea. For example, mint has a refreshing taste, lavender has sweet floral notes, and lemon balm has an earthy, lemony flavor. Each herb adds its special taste to dishes and teas, making cooking and drinking tea an exciting experience.

Common Herbs

Some of the common herbs from the mint family are listed as follows:

- **Mint (Mentha)**: Well-known for its cool, refreshing flavor. Often a star ingredient in a myriad of dishes and a variety of mint teas.
- **Basil (Ocimum Basilicum)**: A staple in Italian cuisine with its sweet and slightly peppery flavor.
- **Rosemary (Rosmarinus Officinalis)**: Popular for its pine-like, earthy flavor. Its essence carries into the realm of aromatic teas.
- **Lavender (Lavandula)**: With a distinct floral aroma and a hint of sweetness. Commonly used in teas for its calming effects.
- **Lemon Balm (Melissa Officinalis)**: Has citrusy, fresh flavor. Known for its calming and soothing properties.
- **Sage (Salvia)**: A classic herb with a long history of culinary and medicinal use.

Rose (Rosaceae) Family

The Rosaceae family is a diverse and economically important family of flowering plants, notable for its many ornamental and fruit-bearing members. The elegance of roses, the sweetness of cherries, and the aroma of hawthorns are all gifts from this large and varied family. Within herbal teas, the Rosaceae family brings a bouquet of flavors and aromas, enhancing our senses with every sip.

Characteristics

The defining features of the Rosaceae family are as numerous as they are fascinating. The family is known for its diverse floral morphology, often exhibiting a classic five-petaled flower, a multitude of stamens, and a characteristic compound ovary. The leaves of

Rosaceae members are usually alternately arranged and often bear stipules, small leaf-like structures at the base of the stalk. These plants often have compound leaves, which means a single leaf is divided into smaller leaflets. The presence of often spiny or prickly stems is another notable characteristic, as anyone who has tried to pluck a wild rose may attest.

Taxonomy of Herbs

Under the botanical classification, the Rosaceae family falls within the order of Rosales. This family is a vast assembly of about 90 genera and over 3,000 species spread across the globe. The family is primarily known for its ornamental plants, fruit-bearing trees, and shrubs. The taxonomy further divides this family into several subfamilies, with Rosoideae and Maloideae being two prominent ones, each housing several genera of economic and ecological importance.

Flavor Profiles

The flavor profiles of herbs and other plants in the Rosaceae family are as varied as their floral displays. The fruits from this family, like apples, pears, and cherries, often offer a sweet, sometimes tart, and always juicy experience. On the other hand, the floral members bring in a range of aromas, from the sweet, classic fragrance of roses to the earthy, subtle scent of potentillas. The herbs, like the burnets, have a cucumber-like flavor, which is refreshing and mild, making them a delightful component in herbal teas.

Common Herbs

Here are some common herbs and other notable members of this family:

- **Roses (Rosa)**: Beyond their ornamental value, roses are a classic ingredient in herbal teas, offering a delicate, sweet flavor and a plethora of health benefits.
- **Burnets (Sanguisorba)**: Known for their mild cucumber-like flavor, burnets are often used in salads and soups and make a refreshing addition to herbal teas.
- **Hawthorns (Crataegus)**: The leaves, flowers, and berries of hawthorn are used in traditional medicine and provide a mild, apple-like flavor to teas.
- **Strawberries (Fragaria)**: While not an herb, strawberries are a beloved member of this family, and their leaves can be used in herbal teas, providing a mild, fruity flavor.
- **Lady's Mantles (Alchemilla)**: The leaves of lady's mantles are often used in herbal teas and have a mild, grassy flavor.
- **Agrimony (Agrimonia)**: With its slightly bitter, astringent taste, agrimony is a traditional herb used in teas for various health benefits.

Onion (Alliaceae) Family

The Alliaceae family, commonly known as the onion family, is a humble yet indispensable group of plants that grace our kitchen counters and garden plots. With their distinctive flavors and aromatic presence, members of this family have been culinary and medicinal companions to humans for millennia.

Characteristics

The Alliaceae family is unique for its organosulfur compounds, which are responsible for the characteristic pungent aroma and flavors of its members. Typically, plants in this family have bulbs as their underground storage organs, which is a distinctive trait. They exhibit a simple, linear leaf arrangement with parallel veins, and the flowers are often arranged in a spherical cluster known as an umbel. The flowers themselves are generally small, six-petaled, and come in a variety of colors, although white and pink hues are common. The seeds are encased in a capsule and are black and angular.

Taxonomy of Herbs

This herb family is categorized under the order Asparagales. It comprises about 18 genera and over 800 species. The genera Allium and Tulbaghia are among the most notable within this family, housing well-known herbs like garlic, onions, and chives. The taxonomy reflects the morphological similarities and evolutionary relationships among these aromatic plants.

Flavor Profiles

The flavor profile of the Alliaceae family is robust and distinctive. The pungency and spiciness attributed to the sulfur compounds are the hallmarks of this family. Each member brings their own unique twist to this pungent baseline. Onions add a sweet, sharp zest, garlic imparts a strong, spicy kick, while chives offer a mild, onion-like flavor. In the context of herbal teas, these flavors can provide a bold, savory note, making the tea experience rich and invigorating.

Common Herbs

Here is a closer look at some common herbs from this family:

- **Garlic (Allium Sativum)**: Known for its strong flavor and medicinal properties, garlic is a staple in many kitchens and is also used in herbal teas for its health benefits.
- **Onion (Allium Cepa)**: Onion, with its sweet yet pungent flavor, is another essential culinary herb. Though not commonly used in teas, it is an interesting choice for those seeking a savory tea flavor.
- **Chives (Allium Schoenoprasum)**: Chives, with their mild, onion-like flavor, can be a delightful addition to herbal teas, especially in blends designed for savory notes.
- **Leeks (Allium Porrum)**: Though more of a vegetable, leeks share the mild, sweet onion flavor and can be used creatively in savory tea blends.
- **Wild Garlic (Allium Ursinum)**: Wild garlic has a milder flavor compared to common garlic and is often used in traditional medicine as well as in herbal teas for its health-promoting properties.

Sunflower (Asteraceae) Family

The Asteraceae family, commonly recognized as the sunflower family, embraces a wide array of herbs that color our gardens with their vibrant blooms and enrich our teas with their diverse flavors. This family, being one of the largest among flowering plants, offers a fascinating journey into the world of herbs, each with its unique character yet sharing a common botanical lineage.

Characteristics

Diving into the characteristics, the Asteraceae family is known for its composite flower structure, which is quite distinctive. A single flower head is a congregation of many small flowers, or florets, making it appear as one large flower. These florets are usually arranged in a central disc, surrounded by ray florets that form the *'petals.'* The leaves can be simple or compound, with a variety of shapes, and are mostly arranged alternately along the stem. Additionally, members of this family often contain milky sap, which can be seen when the stem is broken.

Taxonomy of Herbs

In the taxonomic realm, the Asteraceae family is housed under the order Asterales. It is a grand assembly comprising over 1,620 genera and about 23,600 species. This vast family is further subdivided into tribes and subfamilies, with the tribe Heliantheae housing the sunflowers and tribe Anthemideae being home to chamomile and other medicinal herbs.

Flavor Profiles

The flavor profiles within the Asteraceae family are as diverse as the family itself. From the slightly sweet, apple-like taste of chamomile to the bitter, earthy notes of dandelion and the spicy kick of tarragon, there is a broad spectrum of flavors to be explored. In the context of herbal teas, the herbs from this family provide a range of taste experiences, each with its own unique charm and health benefits, making the tea journey a delightful exploration.

Common Herbs

Acquaint yourself with some common herbs from this family:

- **Chamomile (Matricaria Recutita)**: Known for its gentle, calming properties, chamomile is a star ingredient in many herbal teas, offering a mild, sweet flavor reminiscent of apples.
- **Dandelion (Taraxacum)**: Often seen as a common weed, dandelion is a medicinal powerhouse with a slightly bitter, earthy taste, enriching herbal teas with its detoxifying properties.
- **Tarragon (Artemisia Dracunculus)**: Tarragon, with its spicy, anise-like flavor, adds a zesty note to culinary dishes and herbal teas alike.
- **Calendula (Calendula Officinalis)**: The beautiful orange blossoms of calendula not only add visual appeal but also a mild, peppery flavor to herbal teas.
- **Echinacea (Echinacea Purpurea)**: Known for its immune-boosting properties, Echinacea adds a tingling, numbing sensation to teas, making them truly unique.
- **Yarrow (Achillea Millefolium)**: Yarrow, with its slightly bitter, astringent taste, is a traditional herb often used in teas for its various health benefits.

Mustard (Brassicaceae or Cruciferae) Family

The Brassicaceae or Cruciferae family, often dubbed the mustard family, is a delightful and essential group of plants that play a significant role in our culinary and herbal adventures. Their spiciness adds zest to our meals, and their nutritional bounty contributes to our well-being. In the realm of herbal teas, the unique flavors and health benefits offered by this family can elevate the tea-drinking experience to a new level.

Characteristics

Diving into the characteristics, the members of the Brassicaceae family are known for their cross-like arrangement of four petals and six stamens, which is a distinctive trait. This unique floral arrangement is where the alternative name, Cruciferae, which means *"cross-bearing,"* comes from. The leaves are usually alternately arranged and often have a waxy or hairy texture. The family is also known for its unique seedpods, which come in a variety of shapes and sizes, each housing the seeds in a singular fashion.

Taxonomy of Herbs

The Brassicaceae family finds its place under the order Brassicales, housing about 372 genera and 4,060 known species. This family is quite diverse, hosting a range of plants from tiny herbs to tall trees. The genus Brassica is one of the most notable genera in this family, encompassing many common vegetables and herbs that are integral to our diets.

Flavor Profiles

The flavor profile of the Brassicaceae family is predominantly spicy and peppery, thanks to the presence of mustard oils or glucosinolates, which impart the characteristic pungency. However, each herb and plant in this family carries its unique flavor note, adding a layer of complexity to this spicy baseline. The sharp, peppery kick of mustard greens, the slightly bitter and earthy taste of kale, and the mild spiciness of garden cress are just a glimpse of the flavor palette this family offers.

Common Herbs

Here are some common herbs from this family:

- **Mustard (Brassica Spp.)**: The seeds and leaves of mustard plants are well-loved for their spicy kick and are often used in herbal teas for a warming effect.
- **Garden Cress (Lepidium Sativum)**: Garden cress offers a mild peppery flavor and is a delightful addition to salads and herbal teas alike.
- **Watercress (Nasturtium Officinale)**: The slightly bitter, peppery taste of watercress can add a zing to herbal teas, making them invigorating.
- **Radish (Raphanus Sativus)**: Though more commonly consumed as a vegetable, radish seeds have been used in traditional medicine and can be brewed into a spicy, warming tea.
- **Arugula (Eruca Vesicaria)**: The peppery, nutty flavor of arugula can provide an interesting, spicy note to herbal tea blends.
- **Horseradish (Armoracia Rusticana)**: The strong, pungent flavor of horseradish is unique and can be used sparingly to add a bold kick to herbal teas.

Marshmallow (Malvaceae) Family

The Malvaceae family, charmingly referred to as the marshmallow family, is a delightful collection of plants that embody softness and soothing properties. The gentle whispers of blooms in this family bring along a comforting essence, turning the simple act of tea brewing into a nurturing ritual.

Characteristics

Diving into the characteristics of the Malvaceae family, one is greeted by the soft, often hairy leaves and stems, a feature that imparts a velvety touch to these plants. The flowers, usually exhibiting a beautiful array of five petals, are a soothing sight with their pastel shades of pink, white, and lavender. A distinctive trait is the presence of a column of stamens, forming a tube around the style. The leaves are typically alternate and often have a lobed or palmate shape, adding to the aesthetic charm of these plants.

Taxonomy of Herbs

The Malvaceae family belongs to the order Malvales, encompassing about 244 genera and 4225 known species. This botanical clan is a delightful mix of herbs, shrubs, and trees, each with its unique offering yet bound by the common thread of gentleness and soothing properties. Genus Althaea is particularly notable, housing the marshmallow plant, which lends the family its common name.

Flavor Profiles

The flavor profile of the Malvaceae family is as gentle as its appearance. The mild, sweet, and mucilaginous nature of marshmallow is symbolic of the flavor essence in this family. The mucilage, a type of plant sugar, imparts a sweet, soothing characteristic that is comforting to the palate. In the realm of herbal teas, this sweet, soft essence adds a comforting, smooth quality to the brew.

Common Herbs

Delve into some common herbs from this family:

- **Marshmallow (Althaea officinalis)**: The roots and leaves of marshmallow plants are cherished for their soothing, mucilaginous properties, making them a classic choice for herbal teas aimed at comforting the throat and digestive tract.

- **Hollyhock (Alcea)**: Hollyhocks, with their beautiful blooms, also possess mild soothing properties and can be used in herbal teas.
- **Mallow (Malva)**: Mallow leaves and flowers are known for their mild, sweet flavor and soothing, mucilaginous quality, making them a gentle addition to herbal teas.
- **Okra (Abelmoschus Esculentus)**: Although more of a vegetable, okra's mucilaginous texture is indicative of its family traits. The seeds can be used to create a caffeine-free substitute for coffee.

Bean (Fabaceae) Family

The Fabaceae family, also known as the legume or bean family, is a remarkable group of plants that intertwine with our daily lives in various forms. From the beans on our plate to the beautiful blossoms adorning our gardens and the robust trees shading our paths, this family has a diverse offering. Its contribution extends to the realm of herbal teas, bringing along unique flavors and nutritional richness.

Characteristics

The hallmark of the Fabaceae family is its fruit, typically a pod or legume, which encapsulates seeds in a tender embrace. The leaves are often compound, composed of multiple leaflets, and display a wide range of shapes and arrangements. The flowers, with their unique butterfly-like structure, are not just beautiful but also intriguing. They usually have five petals: an upright standard, two lateral wings, and two lower petals fused together to form a keel. This intricate floral design facilitates specialized pollination, showcasing nature's exquisite engineering.

Taxonomy of Herbs

Belonging to the order Fabales, the Fabaceae family is a grand assembly of about 751 genera and nearly 20,000 species. The family is majorly categorized into three subfamilies: Mimosoideae, known for its fluffy flower heads; Caesalpinioideae, with its unique bilateral symmetrical flowers; and Faboideae, the largest subfamily, housing a myriad of leguminous plants we commonly encounter.

Flavor Profiles

The flavor profiles within the Fabaceae family are as diverse as the family itself. The leguminous members bring forth a nutty, earthy taste, while the floral members lend a sweet, sometimes spicy note. In the context of herbal teas, the flowers and leaves from this family can provide a variety of taste experiences, from the sweet floral taste of red clover to the slightly bitter, earthy flavor of fenugreek seeds.

Common Herbs

Some common herbs from this family:

- **Red Clover (Trifolium Pratense)**: Known for its sweet, grassy flavor, red clover is a popular choice in herbal teas for its health-promoting properties.
- **Fenugreek (Trigonella Foenum-Graecum)**: The seeds of fenugreek offer a slightly sweet, nutty, and somewhat bitter flavor, often used in teas for its many health benefits.
- **Licorice (Glycyrrhiza Glabra)**: The sweet, soothing taste of licorice root is a beloved addition to herbal teas, offering both flavor and health benefits.
- **Astragalus (Astragalus Membranaceus)**: Known for its immune-boosting properties, astragalus root has a sweet, warm flavor, making it a comforting addition to herbal teas.

- **Kudzu (Pueraria Lobata)**: The starchy roots of kudzu are used in traditional medicine and can be brewed into a mild, earthy tea.

Carrot (Apiaceae) Family

The Apiaceae family, commonly known as the carrot or parsley family, is a treasure trove of flavors and textures that have found a cherished place in our kitchens and herbal practices. This family embraces a wide array of plants that add zest to our meals, color to our gardens, and aromatic bliss to our tea rituals.

Characteristics

A dive into the characteristics of the Apiaceae family unveils a fascinating array of features. The plants often exhibit finely divided, feathery leaves that are aromatic, a trait that is a hallmark of this family. The unique flower arrangement, known as an umbel, is another distinctive feature where small flowers spring out from a common point, much like the ribs of an umbrella. These flowers are usually small, but collectively they form a beautiful, flat, or rounded cluster. The fruits are typically small and dry, often splitting into two halves when mature.

Taxonomy of Herbs

The Apiaceae family is nestled under the order Apiales, housing around 434 genera and over 3,700 species. This botanical assembly is a medley of herbs, shrubs, and trees, each with its unique personality yet sharing the family's signature aromatic trait. The genus Daucus, which includes carrots, and the genus Petroselinum, housing parsley, are among the noteworthy genera within this family, showcasing the culinary and medicinal richness it offers.

Flavor Profiles

The flavor profile of the Apiaceae family is as diverse as it is enticing. The sharp, peppery taste of parsley, the sweet earthiness of carrot, and the warm, spicy notes of cumin are just a glimpse of the flavor palette this family presents. In the context of herbal teas, the aromatic and spicy essence of these herbs can invigorate the senses, making the tea experience a delightful journey of flavors.

Common Herbs

Here are some common herbs from this family:

- **Parsley (Petroselinum Crispum)**: Known for its bright, peppery flavor, parsley is not just a garnish but an herb that can add a refreshing zing to herbal teas.
- **Caraway (Carum Carvi)**: The warm, sweet, and slightly peppery flavor of caraway seeds is a delightful addition to herbal teas, lending a comforting, aromatic essence.
- **Cumin (Cuminum Cyminum)**: Cumin's warm, earthy, and spicy flavor is a classic choice for an aromatic, invigorating tea.
- **Coriander (Coriandrum Sativum)**: The sweet, citrusy flavor of coriander seeds can add a refreshing, aromatic note to herbal teas.
- **Fennel (Foeniculum Vulgare)**: The sweet, licorice-like flavor of fennel seeds is cherished in herbal teas for its soothing and aromatic properties.
- **Anise (Pimpinella Anisum)**: With a sweet, licorice-like flavor, anise seeds are a delightful choice for a sweet, aromatic tea.

Sourcing Quality Herbs

The journey towards crafting a delightful and beneficial cup of herbal tea begins long before the kettle whistles. It starts at the source, with the selection of quality herbs.

The Importance of Quality

Quality is not merely a measure of purity and potency but a reflection of the care, ethics, and sustainable practices employed from the seed to the shelf. High-quality herbs are the foundation of effective and enjoyable herbal teas. They ensure that the flavors are rich, the aroma is inviting, and the health benefits are optimized. Moreover, quality sourcing reflects a commitment to environmental sustainability, ethical practices, and social responsibility, embodying a holistic approach toward enjoying the goodness of nature.

Ethical Sourcing

Embarking on the path of ethical sourcing is akin to forging a respectful relationship with nature. It involves choosing herbs that are grown and harvested under environmentally sustainable, socially fair, and economically viable conditions. Ethical sourcing not only contributes to the quality and efficacy of the herbs but also aligns with the ethos of holistic wellness that herbal teas represent.

Quality Evaluation

The art of quality evaluation is a blend of sensory assessment and scientific analysis. It entails evaluating the herbs for their color, texture, aroma, and taste while also ensuring they are free from contaminants and adulterations. High-quality herbs are the essence of herbal teas that are delightful to the senses and beneficial to health.

A Guide to Determining Herb Quality

Determining the quality of herbs is a blend of sensory assessment, information gathering, and, sometimes, lab testing. Here is a guide on how to evaluate the quality of herbs through reputable suppliers:

- **Transparency:** Reputable suppliers are transparent about the origin, cultivation practices, and processing of the herbs they provide. Look for suppliers who provide detailed information about the herbs, including the scientific name, origin, cultivation practices, and any certifications like organic, fair trade, etc.
- **Documentation:** Check for documentation like Certificates of Analysis (CoA), which provide detailed information about the purity, potency, and safety of the herbs.
- **Sensory Evaluation:** High-quality herbs have a vibrant color, fresh aroma, and a clean, unadulterated taste. Reputable suppliers often provide samples for evaluation.
- **Purity Checks:** Inquire about the purity checks the supplier performs to ensure the herbs are free from contaminants like pesticides, heavy metals, and microbial contamination.
- **Ethical Certifications:** Look for certifications like Fair Trade, Organic, or others that align with ethical sourcing and quality standards.
- **Customer Support:** Reputable suppliers are ready to answer your queries, provide further information, and assist you in making informed choices.
- **Reviews and References:** Check reviews, ask for references, and engage with other customers to understand their experience with the supplier.
- **Educational Resources:** Some reputable suppliers provide educational resources to help customers understand the quality, usage, and benefits of the herbs they are purchasing.

Storage and Shelf Life

In the aromatic voyage of herbal teas, the steps from sourcing quality herbs to brewing the perfect cup encompass much more than meets the eye. Among these steps, the storage of herbs and understanding their shelf life are pivotal. Proper storage ensures that the herbs retain their quality, flavor, and health benefits from the moment they are sourced until they are brewed into a comforting cup of tea.

Storage Conditions

The journey of herbs from the field to your cup is long and can be fraught with challenges. One of the key factors that ensure the herbs remain fresh, potent, and beneficial is the conditions under which they are stored.

Why is this Important?

The storage conditions significantly impact the quality, flavor, and efficacy of the herbs. Proper storage ensures that the herbs are protected from factors that could lead to degradation or spoilage, thus ensuring that the cup of herbal tea you brew is rich in flavor and benefits. Aside from this, the potency of herbs, which is the intensity of their flavor and therapeutic properties, can be significantly impacted by how they are stored.

What to Consider?

Below is a quick guide on what to consider to preserve the herb's essence:

- **Temperature:** Store herbs in a cool, dry place away from direct sunlight to prevent the degradation of essential oils and other beneficial compounds.
- **Humidity:** Moisture can be detrimental, leading to mold and spoilage. Ensure herbs are stored in a dry environment.
- **Air Exposure:** Herbs should be stored in airtight containers to prevent oxidation and loss of potency.

- **Light:** Exposure to light can cause herbs to lose their color and potency. Dark glass containers or a dark storage area can mitigate this.

Preventing Spoilage

Herbs, being natural products, are susceptible to spoilage if not stored correctly. Preventing spoilage ensures that the herbs remain safe to consume and retain their intended flavor and therapeutic properties. Do the following to prevent spoilage:

- **Proper Drying:** Before storage, ensure herbs are thoroughly dried to prevent mold and bacterial growth.
- **Airtight Containers:** Store herbs in airtight containers to protect against moisture and air exposure.
- **Regular Checks:** Periodically check stored herbs for signs of spoilage like mold, off-odors, or changes in appearance.
- **Avoiding Cross-contamination:** Store different herbs separately to prevent cross-contamination and mingling of flavors.
- **Temperature Control:** Storing herbs at a consistent, cool temperature can help maintain potency.
- **Avoiding Overexposure:** Limit the exposure of herbs to air, light, and moisture by using appropriate containers and storage areas.
- **Timely Usage:** Herbs do not improve with age, like wine. It is advisable to use them within a specified period to enjoy their maximum potency.

Chapter 4

Techniques of Brewing

Brewing herbal tea is about learning how to get the best flavors and health benefits from herbs and spices by mixing them with water. In this chapter, learn the basics of brewing herbal tea, including choosing the right herbs, what tools you need, and how to develop your taste. Find out how the water temperature, how long you let the tea steep, and the method you use can change the taste and strength of your tea.

The Art of Infusion

Infusion is a time-honored method of extracting the flavors and medicinal properties from plant materials into water, forming the basis of a delightful cup of herbal tea.

Understanding the Basics

Infusion is fundamentally about blending water and herbs in a balanced way. As hot water comes into contact with herbs, it initiates an active exchange. The water serves as a dissolving agent, drawing out the herbs' essential oils, flavors, and therapeutic properties. The process encourages the movement of molecules from the herbs into the water, creating a solution rich in flavor, color, and medicinal properties. Understanding the science behind this dance enhances the ability to control the outcome, leading to a more refined and enjoyable tea experience.

The efficiency of this extraction is affected by several elements, such as the water's temperature, how long the herbs are infused, and the water's quality and cleanliness.

Temperature Matters

Different herbs require different temperatures to release their full spectrum of benefits. While some herbs are more yielding, releasing their essence at a gentle simmer, others demand a more fervent boil to unlock their potential. For instance, delicate herbs like mint or lemon balm may require a lower temperature, while roots and barks may need a higher temperature to extract their beneficial compounds. Mastering the temperature aspect of infusion aids in avoiding over-extraction, which can lead to a bitter or unpleasant taste.

Timing the Infusion

The duration for which the herbs are allowed to infuse also holds significance. A longer infusion time generally allows for a more robust extraction, leading to a stronger flavor and color. However, oversleeping can sometimes result in a bitter brew. Finding the right balance in infusion time is key to achieving the desired strength and flavor in your tea.

Water Quality

Pure, fresh, and clean water is the best canvas for herbal infusion, as it allows the authentic flavors and colors of the herbs to shine through. On the contrary, using impure or chemically treated water can not only distort the taste but also potentially diminish the therapeutic benefits of the herbs.

Tools and Equipment

The tools you choose are more than mere vessels, as they are the gateway to unlocking the full potential of the herbs. Equipping yourself with the right tools and understanding their function in the infusion process is a step towards mastering the art of brewing herbal teas. It is an investment that pays off in the form of enhanced flavors, preserved medicinal properties, and an overall enriched tea-drinking experience.

Teapots

A good-quality teapot is like being a faithful companion in the journey of tea brewing. It houses the interaction between water and herbs, providing the right environment for the infusion to happen. Teapots come in various materials like glass, ceramic, clay, or stainless steel. Each has unique attributes that can influence the flavor and quality of the infusion. For instance, clay teapots are known to absorb flavors over time, adding a depth of taste to the brew, while glass teapots allow you to visually enjoy the infusion process. Make sure your teapot has a well-fitting lid, as it is important in retaining the heat and letting the magic of infusion unfold in a sealed environment.

Infusers

Infusers come in various designs and materials, with the common ones being basket infusers, ball infusers, or silicone infusers. The design of the infuser should allow ample space for the herbs to expand and float, ensuring a well-rounded extraction of flavors and medicinal properties. The size of the holes in the infuser should be small enough to prevent herb particles from escaping into the water yet large enough to allow the water to circulate freely among the herbs.

Strainers

Once your tea has steeped enough, remove the herbs from the water. A fine-mesh strainer works best, catching the herbs and leaving you with a clear tea. Some teapots even have strainers built-in, which makes this step even easier.

Heating Source

The source of heat you use to warm the water for infusion is also a part of the equipment lineup. Whether it is a traditional stove, an electric kettle, or a modern induction cooktop, the goal is to achieve the desired temperature control. Electric kettles with temperature settings are a handy tool for ensuring the water reaches the precise temperature needed for your infusion.

Measuring Tools

Measuring the right quantity of herbs and water is fundamental to achieving a balanced infusion. Having measuring spoons and cups allows you to maintain consistency in your brew, especially when you find the perfect ratio that suits your taste.

Storage Containers

Preserving the freshness and potency of your herbs is essential for a high-quality infusion. Airtight containers that block out light and moisture are ideal for storing both fresh and dried herbs. Proper storage ensures that the herbs retain their medicinal properties and flavor profile until they are ready to be brewed.

Fresh vs. Dried Herbs

The choice between fresh and dried herbs is as important as understanding the infusion process and the tools required for it. Each type comes with its unique set of attributes and uses.

Fresh Herbs

Fresh herbs are the green, aromatic leaves and stems harvested directly from plants. They carry the essence of the garden, embodying a lively and vibrant character. The inherent moisture content in fresh herbs aids in the preservation of their aromatic oils and medicinal compounds, translating into a robust flavor and a rich therapeutic profile.

What to Use

- **Mint:** Fresh mint leaves are a classic choice for infusions, offering a cool, refreshing flavor and a soothing effect on the digestive system.
- **Lemon Balm:** Known for its calming properties, fresh lemon balm adds a mild lemony flavor to teas.
- **Basil:** Fresh basil, especially the sweet or holy varieties, lends a sweet, slightly spicy character to infusions.
- **Rosemary:** With its strong, piney flavor, fresh rosemary can invigorate the senses and enhance mental clarity.
- **Chamomile:** Fresh chamomile flowers offer a sweet, apple-like flavor and a calming, anti-inflammatory effect.

Dried Herbs

Dried herbs are the result of a careful process where fresh herbs are dehydrated to remove moisture, thus preserving their medicinal properties and flavor for extended periods. The drying process concentrates the flavors and active compounds, offering a more potent and shelf-stable alternative to fresh herbs.

What to Use

- **Lavender:** Dried lavender flowers are renowned for their relaxing properties and distinct floral aroma.

- **Echinacea:** Often used to support immune health, dried echinacea can provide a slightly earthy, tingling infusion.
- **Nettle:** Dried nettle leaves offer a rich mineral content and a taste reminiscent of green tea.
- **Dandelion Root:** With its earthy, roasted flavor, dried dandelion root is often used for its detoxifying benefits.
- **Hibiscus:** The dried petals of hibiscus provide a tart, cranberry-like flavor, and a vibrant red color to infusions.

Deciding Between Fresh and Dried Herbs

The decision between fresh and dried herbs is a personal one, influenced by various factors, including taste preferences, availability, desired medicinal benefits, and lifestyle considerations. By understanding the nuances between fresh and dried herbs, you empower yourself to make choices that enhance your infusion journey, allowing you to explore and enjoy the vast spectrum of flavors and health benefits that herbal teas offer.

The choice between fresh and dried herbs for your tea mainly depends on the taste and smell you want. Fresh herbs give a lively, natural flavor and a strong, fresh scent, like a garden in full bloom. Dried herbs have a stronger, more concentrated taste and a milder, earthier smell.

Availability and Seasonality

The availability of fresh herbs may be limited by seasonal and geographic constraints. If you have a herb garden or live in a region where herbs grow abundantly, fresh herbs might be a readily accessible choice. Conversely, dried herbs provide a year-round, consistent option regardless of seasonal changes.

Medicinal Value

Fresh and dried herbs possess medicinal properties, yet the concentration of beneficial compounds may vary. Drying herbs can concentrate certain compounds, potentially offering a more potent medicinal brew. Some volatile compounds, however, may be lost during the drying process, which might be retained in fresh herbs.

Storage and Shelf Life

Dried herbs have a longer shelf life and are easier to store, making them a convenient choice for those without regular access to fresh herbs. Yet, fresh herbs require refrigeration and should be used promptly to ensure they retain their flavor and medicinal properties.

Practicality

Dried herbs are convenient for busy people or those without easy access to fresh herbs. These herbs do not need any preparation and can last longer, allowing you to buy them in bulk and use them whenever you want.

Experimentation

Try both fresh and dried herbs to see what you like best. Each type gives a different taste and health benefit, making your tea brewing experience more varied and enjoyable.

Dried Tea Recipes

Discover the rich flavors and aromas of dried teas, which last longer and have more intense ingredients. These recipes showcase the variety and depth of dried teas, each designed to bring out the best in dried herbs, flowers, and leaves:

Soothing Rose and Hibiscus Tea

A floral and citrusy blend, ideal for relaxation. The dried ingredients offer a concentrated flavor and longer shelf-life compared to fresh counterparts.

Ingredients:

- 1 tbsp dried rose petals
- 1 tbsp dried hibiscus flowers
- 1 tsp dried orange peel
- Honey or sugar *(optional)*

Instructions:

1. Combine dried rose petals, hibiscus flowers, and orange peel in a tea infuser or loose in a pot.
2. Pour boiling water over the mix and steep for 5 to 7 minutes.
3. Strain into a cup, and sweeten with honey or sugar if desired.

Minty Rooibos Delight

A refreshing and soothing tea with a natural sweetness. The dried peppermint is more potent and less perishable than fresh mint.

Ingredients:

- 1 tbsp dried rooibos tea
- 1 tsp dried peppermint leaves
- A pinch of dried stevia leaves *(for natural sweetness)*

Instructions:

1. Blend dried rooibos and peppermint leaves together.
2. Steep the blend in hot water for 5 minutes.

3. Add a pinch of dried stevia leaves for sweetness, strain, and serve.

Spiced Dandelion Chai

Earthy and spicy, this chai uses dried dandelion for a robust, longer-lasting flavor compared to fresh roots.

Ingredients:

- 1 tbsp dried dandelion root
- 1/2 tsp dried ginger powder
- 1/4 tsp ground cinnamon
- 1/4 tsp ground cardamom
- 1/4 tsp ground cloves
- Milk and honey *(to taste)*

Instructions:

1. Combine dandelion root, ginger powder, cinnamon, cardamom, and cloves.
2. Add the mixture to boiling water and simmer for 10 minutes.
3. Strain into a cup, and add milk and honey to taste.

Calming Lavender and Chamomile Blend

A gentle, soothing tea perfect for relaxation. Dried chamomile and lavender have an intensified aroma and are more convenient than fresh herbs.

Ingredients:

- 1 tbsp dried chamomile flowers
- 1 tsp dried lavender buds
- 1 tsp dried lemon balm leaves

Instructions:

1. Mix chamomile, lavender, and lemon balm in a teapot.
2. Pour boiling water over the herbs and steep for 10 minutes.
3. Strain and enjoy the calming effects.

Berry Bliss Tea

A fruity and tangy blend, rich in antioxidants. Dried berries retain their flavor and nutrients longer than fresh berries, making them ideal for tea.

Ingredients:

- 1 tbsp dried elderberries
- 1 tbsp dried blueberries
- 1 tsp dried hibiscus flowers
- Honey or sugar *(optional)*

Instructions:

1. Mix elderberries, blueberries, and hibiscus in a teapot or infuser.
2. Pour boiling water over the berries and steep for 7 to 10 minutes.
3. Strain and add honey or sugar if desired.

Green Tea & Jasmine Harmony

A serene and aromatic fusion, this tea marries the subtle, refreshing qualities of green tea with the sweet, intoxicating aroma of jasmine.

Ingredients:

- 1 tbsp dried green tea leaves
- 1 tsp dried jasmine flowers
- A slice of fresh ginger or a pinch of lemon zest *(optional)*

Instructions:

1. Mix green tea leaves and jasmine flowers in a teapot.
2. Pour boiling water over the mixture and steep for 3 minutes.
3. For an additional twist, add a slice of fresh ginger or a pinch of lemon zest.
4. Strain and serve, savoring the delicate balance of green tea and jasmine.

Decoctions and Tisanes

Exploring herbal teas introduces you to different ways of brewing, each bringing out unique flavors and benefits. Two important methods are decoctions and tisanes, which help extract goodness from herbs, roots, and other plants.

Decoctions

Decoctions are a key part of herbal traditions. This method is great for getting the most out of tough plant parts like roots, bark, and seeds. Decoctions bring out deep flavors and strong healing properties that lighter teas might not have.

Why Decoctions?

Unlike simple infusions, where herbs are steeped in hot water, decoction involves simmering these materials in water over a period. This slow extraction process allows for a more potent brew, often unveiling deeper flavors and more profound medicinal benefits. It is a method that appreciates the time it takes for a deep communion between water and plant matter, resulting in a brew that is rich in both taste and therapeutic benefits.

The Process

To grasp the concept of decoction, imagine it as a gentle yet effective method to access the powerful properties of medicinal plants. The process starts simply: take the plant parts—like roots or barks—and chop them to expose more surface area. Place these coarsely chopped materials in a pot with water, cover it with a lid, and let it simmer slowly. This simmering can vary from a brief 20 minutes to several hours, depending on the type of plant you are using. It is a patient method where the plants gradually yield their beneficial compounds to the warm water.

Benefits

Decoctions excel in extracting heavier constituents such as alkaloids, tannins, and other robust compounds from tougher plant materials, which lighter infusions might leave behind. This is especially significant when brewing herbs for their medicinal benefits. For example, the roots of herbs like burdock or dandelion, known for their liver-supportive properties, give up their medicinal compounds readily in a decoction. The result is a potent brew that carries the therapeutic promise of the herbs deep within.

Choice of Materials

Not all plant materials are suited for decoction. It is the tougher, more resilient parts like roots, barks, seeds, and some herbs with robust fibers that stand up well to the simmering process of decoction. Examples include astragalus root, known for its immune-boosting properties; cinnamon bark, with its warming and blood sugar-balancing effects; and fenugreek seeds, which are often used to support digestive and hormonal health.

Tisanes

Unlike green, black, white, and oolong teas, which come from the Camellia sinensis plant, tisanes are made from a wide variety of ingredients, such as leaves, petals, fruits, seeds, and spices. Tisanes offer a different range of flavors and properties, and a gentle brewing process extracts the subtle essences and benefits of each botanical.

Why Tisanes?

Tisanes are simple to make because they require less heat and less time than decoctions, making them ideal for using soft parts of plants like leaves, petals, and aromatic herbs. Unlike many tea infusions, tisanes do not contain caffeine. With every sip of a tisane, you get to enjoy the mild flavors and soothing effects of the plants. Such gentle qualities and lack of caffeine set them apart as a calm and special option among herbal drinks.

The Process Explored

Start by choosing your ingredients, which can be anything from the gentle calm of chamomile blossoms to the refreshing kick of mint leaves or even the tangy zest of citrus rinds. Once you have selected your mix, you simply pour hot water over them and let them sit. This steeping is not as intense as the simmer needed for decoctions; it is a relaxed affair where the heat slowly encourages the plants to infuse their qualities into the water. How long you steep them depends on your personal taste and the herbs you are using—generally, it is about 5 to 15 minutes.

Benefits

A lavender tisane, for example, might be the perfect companion for unwinding after a long day, thanks to its calming properties.

Reach for a ginger tisane, and you can find comfort in its warmth and support for digestion.

When it comes to taste, tisanes are a delightfully varied bunch. Imagine relishing the sweet, aromatic caress of rose petals, the crisp freshness of mint, or the bold, warming zing of cinnamon. Each ingredient in a tisane brings its own unique flavor party to your cup, making every sip a new and exciting experience.

Choice of Botanicals

Each botanical selected for a tisane comes with its own story and set of characteristics. Chamomile flowers, for instance, are famed for their gentle, honeyed touch that can ease you into relaxation. Lemon balm leaves, on the other hand, bring a refreshing citrus note that's both uplifting and comforting. With such a variety of plants to choose from, you can tailor your tisane to fit exactly what you are in the mood for—whether that is something to soothe, energize, or satisfy a particular flavor craving.

Which to Choose?

When you are torn between making a tisane or a decoction, think about the plants you are working with and the kind of drink you want to create. *Are you aiming for a medicinal drink or a soothing, fragrant cup?*

A decoction is the way to go if your cupboard is full of tough roots, thick barks, or whole seeds. This method is great for releasing the strong flavors and healing properties of these hardy ingredients into a powerful liquid. Decoctions take time and heat to create a rich and beneficial drink.

Try making a tisane when you prefer something lighter and more fragrant. A tisane gently brings out a variety of flavors and health benefits. It is the right choice when you want a soothing and relaxing cup that highlights the subtle complexities of each ingredient.

Exploring Herbal Decoctions and Tisanes Recipes

Explore the strong teas made from boiling tough plant parts like roots and barks and the gentle teas made from steeping leaves, flowers, and herbs.

Decoction

Recipes for decoctions are as follows:

Burdock Root and Ginger Decoction

This decoction combines the earthy, deep flavors of burdock root with the spicy warmth of fresh ginger. Burdock root is celebrated for its blood-purifying and detoxifying properties, while ginger adds a zesty, digestive-aiding component. The simmering process intensifies their medicinal qualities, making this decoction a robust and healthful drink.

Ingredients:

- 1 tbsp chopped burdock root
- 1-inch piece of fresh ginger, sliced
- 4 cups of water

Instructions:

1. Combine burdock root and ginger in a pot with water.
2. Bring to a boil, then simmer for 30 minutes.
3. Strain and serve warm. This decoction is known for its detoxifying properties and can aid in digestion.

Cinnamon and Star Anise Decoction

Aromatic and sweetly spiced, this decoction is a blend of cinnamon and star anise, both known for their warming properties. Cinnamon brings a comforting sweetness and is known to help with blood sugar regulation, while star anise adds a licorice-like depth, aiding in digestion and respiratory health. It is a perfect soothing beverage for chilly evenings or as a digestive aid.

Ingredients:

- 2 sticks of cinnamon
- 3 star anise pods
- 4 cups of water

Instructions:

1. Place cinnamon and star anise in a pot with water.
2. Boil and then simmer for 20 minutes.
3. Strain and enjoy either hot or cold. This decoction offers a warming and soothing effect, perfect for colder days.

Licorice and Fennel Digestive Decoction

Licorice root adds a natural sweetness and is known for its anti-inflammatory properties, while fennel seeds bring a refreshing and slightly spicy flavor, often used to alleviate bloating and digestive discomfort.

Ingredients:

- 1 tsp licorice root
- 1 tsp fennel seeds
- 4 cups water

Instructions:

1. Combine licorice root and fennel seeds in a pot with water.
2. Bring to a boil, then simmer for 25 minutes.
3. Strain and serve. This decoction is known for aiding digestion and soothing stomach ailments.

Valerian and Hops Sleep Aid Decoction

This decoction is a natural sleep aid, combining the sedative effects of valerian root and hops. Valerian root is widely used for its ability to improve sleep quality and promote relaxation, while hops add to the calming effect, helping to ease insomnia. The gentle simmering process melds these herbs into a potent brew that is perfect for sipping before bedtime to encourage a peaceful night's rest.

Ingredients:

- 1 tsp valerian root
- 1 tsp hops
- 4 cups water

Instructions:

1. Combine valerian root and hops in a pot with water.
2. Bring to a boil, then simmer for 20 minutes.
3. Strain and drink before bedtime. This decoction is known for its sedative properties, promoting restful sleep.

Nettle and Horsetail Mineral-Rich Decoction

Rich in minerals, this decoction brings together nettle leaves and horsetail, both of which are renowned for their nutrient content. Nettle is a powerhouse of vitamins and minerals, particularly helpful for skin and hair health, while horsetail is known for its silica content, supporting bone and hair strength. This mineral-packed decoction is ideal for anyone looking to boost their overall

Ingredients:

- 1 tbsp dried nettle leaves
- 1 tbsp horsetail
- 4 cups water

Instructions:

1. Place nettle leaves and horsetail in a pot with water.
2. Boil and then simmer for 25 minutes.
3. Strain and drink to benefit from their high mineral content, which is particularly useful for bone and hair health.

Hawthorn Berry Heart Health Decoction

Focused on cardiovascular wellness, this decoction utilizes the benefits of hawthorn berries, known for their heart-supportive properties. Hawthorn berries are believed to improve circulation, regulate blood pressure, and enhance heart function. The extended simmering allows the extraction of these beneficial compounds, resulting in a decoction that not only supports heart health but also has a pleasant, slightly fruity flavor.

Ingredients:

- 2 tbsp dried hawthorn berries
- 4 cups water

Instructions:

1. Combine hawthorn berries with water in a pot.
2. Bring to a boil, then simmer for 35 to 40 minutes.
3. Strain and enjoy to support cardiovascular health.

Tisane Recipes

While here are recipes if you would like to make a tisane.

Rosehip and Hibiscus Vitamin C Tisane

This tisane is a vibrant blend of rosehips and hibiscus, both rich in Vitamin C and antioxidants. The rosehips provide a tangy, fruity flavor, complemented by the tart, cranberry-like taste of hibiscus. It is not only a healthful drink but also a visually stunning one, with a deep, ruby-red color.

Ingredients:

- 2 tbsp dried rosehips
- 1 tbsp dried hibiscus flowers
- 2 cups boiling water

Instructions:

1. Place rosehips and hibiscus in a teapot or infuser.
2. Pour boiling water over them and steep for 10 to 15 minutes.
3. Strain and enjoy either hot or cold. This tisane is rich in Vitamin C and antioxidants.

Lemon Verbena and Ginger Soothing Tisane

Combining the refreshing, citrusy notes of lemon verbena with the spicy warmth of ginger, this tisane is both soothing and invigorating. Ideal for calming an upset stomach or relaxing after a meal, it offers a zesty and slightly spicy flavor profile that is both comforting and uplifting.

Ingredients:

- 1 tbsp dried lemon verbena leaves

- 1-inch piece of fresh ginger, thinly sliced
- 2 cups boiling water

Instructions:

1. Combine lemon verbena and ginger in a teapot or infuser.
2. Add boiling water and steep for 5 to 10 minutes.
3. Strain and serve. This tisane is excellent for soothing the throat and calming the stomach.

Chamomile and Lavender Tisane

This tisane is a serene blend of chamomile and lavender, both renowned for their calming and relaxing effects. Chamomile offers a mildly sweet and floral flavor, often used to alleviate stress and promote sleep. Lavender adds a soothing, aromatic touch, making this tisane ideal for unwinding at the end of the day.

Ingredients:

- 1 tbsp dried chamomile flowers
- 1 tsp dried lavender buds
- 2 cups of boiling water

Instructions:

1. Place chamomile and lavender in a teapot or infuser.
2. Pour boiling water over the herbs and steep for 10 minutes.
3. Strain and drink before bedtime for a calming effect.

Peppermint and Lemon Balm Tisane

Refreshing and invigorating, this tisane melds the cool, minty notes of peppermint with the subtle, citrusy undertones of lemon balm. Peppermint is a fantastic digestive aid, while lemon balm is known for its calming effects on the mind and body. This blend is perfect for soothing the digestive system or for simply enjoying a refreshing, caffeine-free pick-me-up.

Ingredients:

- 1 tbsp dried peppermint leaves
- 1 tsp dried lemon balm
- 2 cups of boiling water

Instructions:

1. Combine peppermint and lemon balm in a teapot or infuser.
2. Add boiling water and steep for 5 to 7 minutes.
3. Strain and enjoy. This tisane is refreshing and can help in soothing digestive discomfort.

Blueberry and Mint Refreshing Tisane

This tisane is a delightful blend, perfect for hot days. The dried blueberries offer a rich source of antioxidants, while the mint provides a refreshing and cooling flavor. Sweeten to your liking for a rejuvenating, antioxidant-rich drink.

Ingredients:

- 1 tbsp dried blueberries
- 1 tbsp fresh mint leaves *(or 1 tsp dried)*
- 2 cups boiling water
- Sweetener of choice *(optional)*

Instructions:

1. Combine blueberries and mint in a teapot or infuser.
2. Add boiling water and steep for 7 to 10 minutes.
3. Strain and sweeten if desired.

Cardamom and Rose Relaxing Tisane

Ideal for relaxation and stress relief. The cardamom offers a sweet, spicy aroma, while the rose petals bring a floral and calming quality. It is a perfect choice for unwinding after a long day.

Ingredients:

- 1 tsp crushed cardamom pods
- 1 tbsp dried rose petals
- 2 cups boiling water
- Honey or sweetener of choice *(optional)*

Instructions:

1. Mix cardamom and rose petals in a teapot or infuser.
2. Pour boiling water over them and steep for 5 to 8 minutes.
3. Strain and add honey or sweetener as desired.

Apple and Cinnamon Comforting Tisane

The combination of sweet apples and aromatic cinnamon creates a cozy, comforting beverage. It is perfect for chilly evenings or whenever you need a warming, soothing drink.

Ingredients:

- 1 tbsp dried apple pieces
- 1 cinnamon stick *(or 1 tsp ground cinnamon)*
- 2 cups boiling water
- Sweetener of choice *(optional)*

Instructions:

1. Add dried apple pieces and cinnamon to a teapot or infuser.

2. Pour boiling water over the ingredients and steep for 10 to 12 minutes.
3. Strain and sweeten as desired.

Lemongrass and Basil Energizing Tisane

The lemongrass offers a citrusy, fresh flavor, while the basil contributes a slightly sweet, peppery taste. It is an excellent choice for a natural pick-me-up during your day.

Ingredients:

- 1 tbsp fresh lemongrass *(or 1 tsp dried)*
- 1 tbsp fresh basil leaves *(or 1 tsp dried)*
- 2 cups boiling water

Instructions:

1. Place lemongrass and basil in a teapot or infuser.
2. Pour boiling water over the herbs and steep for 5 to 7 minutes.
3. Strain and enjoy.

Tasting Notes

Having explored the gentle art of tisanes and the deeper extraction process of decoctions, the following sections will further unfold the vast panorama of herbal teas. Immersing in the tasting notes will further enrich your understanding and appreciation of the diverse world of herbal brews. It is like learning a new language that enables you to articulate the symphony of flavors and aromas in every cup of tea.

Developing a Tea Palate

Much like the painter discerns subtle hues in a sunset or a musician detects the delicate notes in a melody, a tea enthusiast can cultivate a palate to explore the myriad flavors and aromas nestled in each tea leaf. Developing a tea palate is a voyage of sensory discovery, a fine-tuning of your senses to the whimsical world of flavors and aromas that each brew encapsulates.

Steps to Develop a Tea Palate

Do the following to enhance your tea palate:

- **Exploration:** Begin with an exploration of the wide array of teas. Each type, be it a black tea, a delicate white tea, or a myriad of herb and floral tisanes, has a unique palette of flavors and aromas to offer.
- **Observation:** Engage all your senses. Observe the color of the brew, inhale the aroma, and delve into the taste. *Is it floral, fruity, earthy, spicy, or nutty?* Each sip is a narrative waiting to be understood.
- **Documentation:** Maintain a tea journal. Document your observations, your likes, and dislikes. Note the flavors, the aromas, and how they made you feel. Over time, this journal will reflect your evolving palate.
- **Comparison:** Compare different teas side by side. Understand the contrasts and appreciate the similarities. It is in comparison that the distinct character of each tea shines through.
- **Education:** Educate yourself about the teas you are tasting. Understand the origin, the processing, and the traditional tasting notes associated with each tea. Knowledge enhances appreciation.
- **Mindful Tasting:** Practice mindful tasting. Immerse in the experience, free from distractions. Let each tasting

be a moment of mindfulness, a meditative delve into the essence of the brew.

- **Tasting Events and Workshops:** Participate in tea-tasting events and workshops. Learning from others, sharing experiences, and tasting curated selections under guidance can significantly enhance your palate.
- **Feedback:** Seek feedback from seasoned tea tasters and engage in discussions.

Complementary Food Pairings

In the culinary universe, the art of pairing the right flavors can turn a simple meal into an unforgettable feast. This magic of pairing extends into the world of tea, where the right snack can turn a tea break into a full-blown sensory journey. Exploring different teas and learning which foods to pair them with can deepen your appreciation and amplify the pleasure of every cup.

The Science Behind Pairing

The secret to a successful pairing is all about balance and harmony in the sensory attributes of both the tea and its accompanying food. Scientifically, what you are aiming for is a complementary or contrasting profile that either amplifies or balances the flavors in your cup of tea.

Taste buds can detect five basic tastes – sweet, salty, sour, bitter, and umami. A well-paired tea and food combo will engage these tastes in a way that one enhances or contrasts with the other. For example, the bitterness in a black tea can be beautifully offset by the sweetness of a scone or a piece of dark chocolate, leading to a more rounded and pleasing taste experience. The contrasting flavors interact on the palate, each one tempering the extremes of the other.

Additionally, it is not only about taste—aroma, temperature, and texture play roles, too. A tea's aroma can be altered by the scent of the food, while the temperature of the drink can affect the texture and flavor release of the food. When these elements are carefully considered, you end up with a pairing that elevates both the tea and the food, engaging all your senses and making the experience far more enjoyable.

Exploring the Art of Tea Pairing

Explore various pairings from the classic to the exotic, each designed to complement or intriguingly contrast with your brew. From the comforting alliance of chamomile tea with buttery pastries to the bold dance between spicy teas and rich dark chocolate, these examples offer a roadmap to enhancing your next tea moment.

- **Classic Pairings**: These combinations are time-honored favorites, promising a pairing that is as familiar as it is delicious.
    - **Chamomile Tea and Light Pastries:** The soothing apple-like nuances of chamomile tea find their perfect match in the light, flaky textures of buttery pastries.
    - **Green Tea and Sushi:** The fresh, vegetal tones of green tea seamlessly slice through the umami-rich flavors of sushi for a clean, palate-cleansing effect.
- **Adventurous Pairings:** These adventurous selections are for those looking to experiment and excite their palates with contrasting and compelling flavors.
    - **Spicy Herbal Teas and Dark Chocolate:** A daring duo where the warmth of spices in herbal teas meets the complex bitterness of dark chocolate, awakening the senses.

    - **Mint Tea and Lamb:** The cooling whispers of mint tea provide a refreshing counterpoint to the savory depth of lamb, creating a pairing that is as refreshing as it is satisfying.
- **Exotic Pairings:** These exotic combinations promise to transport your senses to far-off lands, offering a new perspective on the art of tea pairing.
    - **Chai Tea and Curry:** A vibrant dance of spices, this pairing marries the bold character of chai with the equally spirited flavors of a rich curry.
    - **Lavender Tea and Lemon Cake:** The elegant floral bouquet of lavender tea pairs delightfully with the bright zest of lemon cake, offering a sophisticated and uplifting experience.

Pairing and Tasting Notes

Learning about the flavors and smells in tea is key to matching it with food. These tasting notes help you spot the special tastes in each tea, like the fresh taste of green tea or the warm spice in chai. They guide you in finding the perfect food match. For example, a tea that tastes like citrus goes well with dark chocolate, making both taste better together. Paying attention to these flavors improves your taste and helps you make exciting and well-matched food and tea combos. So, watch these details as you explore the fun world of mixing tea with food.

Organizing a Tea Tasting Event

Tea, with its ancient roots and diverse palette of flavors, serves as a beautiful medium to bring people together. A tea-tasting event is a celebration of the cultural and botanical richness that each brew encapsulates.

Tasting Notes and Tea Tasting Events

Tasting notes can transform a tea-tasting event from a simple gathering to an educational and sensory-rich experience. By highlighting the distinct flavors and aromas present in each tea, tasting notes provide guests with a roadmap to navigate the complexities of the brews before them.

When you introduce tasting notes into a tea-tasting event, you elevate the engagement. Participants become detectives, identifying hints of fruit, whispers of spice, or the earthiness that lingers after each sip. This interactive element encourages conversation and allows for a shared experience that goes beyond the mere act of drinking tea.

Moreover, these notes are a game changer in cultivating appreciation for the delicate craft of tea making. They can reveal the influence of terroir, the art of blending, and the mastery of processing, all of which contribute to the tea's final character. Guests leave not only with the memory of flavors but also with a deeper understanding of what goes into crafting the teas they enjoy.

Components of a Successful Tea Tasting Event

Hosting a tea-tasting event is a delightful and immersive experience that transcends mere sipping. It is a gathering where enthusiasts and newcomers alike can share in the timeless tradition of tea. As the host, you are the conductor of a symphony where each note is a flavor, each harmony is a blend, and the audience is your guests, each ready to be taken on a sensory journey. Your role is to curate an environment where the complexities of tea can be appreciated, where the stories of distant lands and ancient practices come alive with each pour, and where a community can be woven together by the shared passion for the world's most beloved beverage. Listed below are steps for hosting your own tea-tasting event.

- **Decide on the Selection of Teas:** Your choice of teas is the cornerstone of the event. Select a diverse range to offer a broad spectrum of flavors and experiences. Includes a variety of teas, from robust black teas to delicate white teas, and a rainbow of herbal tisanes showcasing different herbs, spices, and flowers.
- **Prepare Tasting Cards:** Have tasting cards with brief notes about each tea's origin, flavor profile, and any unique brewing instructions that will make your guests appreciate the teas better. These cards serve as a roadmap for your attendees, guiding them through the tasting journey.
- **Show Your Brewing Equipment:** Ensure you have the right brewing equipment to showcase the brewing process and serve the teas in a manner that retains their character.
- **Have Good Food Pairings:** Arrange complementary food pairings that enhance the tasting experience. You can follow the guidelines discussed in the previous segment on complementary food pairings to select the right bites that harmonize with the teas being tasted.
- **Encourage Interactive Discussions:** Encourage interactive discussions among attendees. Share tasting notes, personal experiences, and observations. It is through sharing that the event becomes a rich learning and enjoyable experience for all.
- **Ambiance:** Create a soothing and inviting ambiance. The setting, music, and decor should enhance the focus on tea and encourage relaxed interactions.
- **Documentation:** Provide attendees with a takeaway, be it a small sample of tea, a booklet of tea facts, or a feedback form to share their experiences and suggestions for future events.

Chapter 5

Herbal Teas for Wellness

In this chapter, you will explore the expansive world of herbal teas and their potential to enhance wellness. The journey begins by understanding how certain herbal brews can help calm the mind and body amidst the stresses of daily life. Then, discover how to craft a relaxing nightly tea routine and try soothing stress-busting recipes. Learn also how to harness antiviral and antibacterial herbs to gently support immunity through delicious infusions.

Stress-Busting Brews

Herbal teas have long been a refuge for those seeking calm amidst the storm of modern life. The gentle steam rising from a cup of carefully chosen herbs can act as a form of relaxation in your hectic days.

Physiology of Stress

Stress is a common phenomenon, yet it is often misunderstood. It is the body's natural defense against threats, preparing you to react swiftly in times of danger. However, the modern world subjects individuals to a continuous stress trigger, which, over time, can lead to chronic stress. This form of stress is not only detrimental to one's mental health but can also cause significant physical health problems such as heart disease, digestive issues, and immune system suppression.

When you encounter a stressful situation, your body responds by releasing stress hormones such as cortisol and adrenaline. These hormones cause a rise in heart rate, blood pressure, and energy supplies to respond to the perceived threat. In the short term, this stress response can be lifesaving. However, when this state of alertness becomes the norm, it is a problem.

Understanding this is important because it lays the groundwork for why and how certain herbal teas can be beneficial. These teas can act as a counterbalance to the stress response. They often contain compounds that can interact with the body's neurochemistry to promote relaxation and alleviate anxiety symptoms.

For example, the soothing warmth and gentle aromas of herbal teas can also provide a sensory counter to stress, promoting a sense of calmness. Herbs like chamomile have properties that can bind to certain brain receptors the same way some anti-anxiety medications do. The act of preparing and sipping tea can also be a form of mindfulness, a much-needed break from the whirlpool of daily stressors.

The interplay between stress and the body's physiology is as important as it is interesting. Being knowledgeable on the underpinnings of stress can help you better appreciate the simple yet effective role herbal teas can play in promoting a calmer and more balanced state of mind and body.

Nightly Tea Routine

Having tea before bed is a moment for yourself. This routine helps you leave behind stress and find calm before you sleep. Plus, drinking tea at night can help you sleep better. It signals to your body that it is time to relax, leading to a more regular sleep pattern.

Choosing the Right Tea

The choice of tea for your nightly ritual is as important as establishing the routine. While black or green tea might be your go-to brew in the morning, these teas contain caffeine that could interfere with sleep. Herbal teas, on the other hand, are usually a safer bet for evening consumption due to their lack of caffeine. Each of these herbal teas brings a unique flavor and set of calming properties to your evening routine, setting the stage for a restful night.

- **Chamomile**: Known for its calming and anti-anxiety properties, chamomile tea is a classic choice for promoting relaxation and better sleep.
- **Lavender**: Lavender tea not only has a delightful aroma but also possesses properties that can alleviate anxiety and promote sleep.
- **Lemon Balm**: Acts as a mild sedative, helping to calm the mind and encourage sleep.
- **Valerian Root**: Used for its sleep-inducing properties, making it a solid choice for a nightly brew.

Crafting Your Routine

To create a soothing prelude to a restful night's sleep, helping you unwind and prepare for the next day, do the following:

1. **Set the Scene:** Dim the lights in your kitchen or wherever you choose to brew your tea. Perhaps light a few candles to soften the atmosphere further, allowing the flicker of the flame to cast a soothing glow around the room. Silence can be golden, but if you prefer some background, consider playing gentle, ambient music or nature sounds that can help quieten your mind.

2. **Timing is Key:** Enjoy your tea 30 to 60 minutes before bed to allow for relaxation. It gives the body time to absorb the calming herbs and for you to slow down.
3. **Prepare the Tea:** Heat water to the appropriate temperature and measure out the tea. Different teas have different requirements, but for most herbal teas, water just off the boil is perfect.
4. **Mindful Brewing:** Measure the tea carefully, considering the strength you desire and the instructions given by the tea maker. Place the tea in a strainer or teapot, or use a tea bag if you prefer. When the water reaches the perfect temperature, pour it over the tea with a slow, deliberate movement. Watch as the water changes color, absorbing the essence of the herbs.
5. **Practice Mindfulness:** Sit down with your back straight and your hands wrapped around the cup or pot, feeling the warmth seeping through the ceramic. Close your eyes and take deep breaths. Inhale for four counts, hold for seven, and exhale for eight. Repeat this breathing exercise until your tea is ready, usually between five to ten minutes, depending on the type of tea.
6. **Strain and Savor:** Strain the tea into your cup and appreciate the warmth and aroma.
7. **Find Your Zen:** Wrap yourself in a blanket if the night is cool. Avoid electronic devices; the blue light can disturb your circadian rhythm, and the goal is to distance yourself from the day's stimulation. Instead, you might choose to read a few pages from a book or simply sit in contemplation, savoring the flavor of the tea and the calmness of the moment.
8. **Relax and Unwind:** As you sip your tea, feel it warming your body and calming your mind. Allow any lingering thoughts from the day to drift away with each exhale. Let the tea calm your body and mind, letting go of the day's stresses.

9. **Reflect and Clean Up:** Spend a few moments in peaceful contemplation before cleaning up.
10. **Prepare for Sleep:** Feel the calmness enveloping you, signaling that it is time to rest.

Benefits

A nightly tea routine can have several benefits:

- **Improved Sleep Quality**: The calming properties of certain herbal teas can promote better sleep quality.
- **Stress Reduction**: The ritual of preparing and enjoying a calming brew can act as a stress-reducing practice, a time to unwind and reflect.
- **Mindfulness**: Preparing and sipping tea can be a form of mindfulness, a way to be present in the moment.

Herbal Tea Recipes

Each blend below follows uncomplicated procedures to unlock and prepare them: combine the ingredients in a teapot or tea infuser, pour boiling water over them, steep for about 10 to 15 minutes, and then strain before enjoying.

Simple Starters

The world of herbal teas is vast, but starting with simple, easily accessible ingredients can be the first step towards embracing this wellness practice. Below are some easy-to-follow recipes to get you started:

Chamomile Lavender Tea

Drift into tranquility with the serene embrace of chamomile and a whisper of fragrant lavender.

Ingredients:

- 2 tablespoons dried chamomile flowers
- 1 tablespoon dried lavender buds
- 2 cups boiling water

Peppermint Lemon Balm Tea

Refresh and calm your senses with the minty zest of peppermint and the soft, citrusy undertones of lemon balm.

Ingredients:

- 2 tablespoons dried peppermint leaves
- 2 tablespoons dried lemon balm leaves
- 2 cups boiling water

Exotic Infusions

For those looking to explore a bit further, exotic blends can offer a new dimension of flavor and wellness benefits.

Tulsi Rose Tea

Indulge in the sacred harmony of tulsi paired with the delicate caress of a rose for a truly spiritual unwind.

Ingredients:

- 2 tablespoons dried tulsi *(holy basil)* leaves
- 1 tablespoon dried rose petals
- 2 cups boiling water

Chai Spiced Herbal Tea

A warm and comforting blend of rooibos and classic chai spices, offering a caffeine-free twist on traditional chai.

Ingredients:

- 1 tablespoon dried rooibos leaves
- 1/2 teaspoon cinnamon
- 1/2 teaspoon cardamom
- 1/4 teaspoon cloves
- 1/4 teaspoon ginger powder
- 2 cups boiling water

Lemongrass and Coconut Tropical Tea

This refreshing blend of zesty lemongrass and sweet coconut offers a taste of the tropics.

Ingredients:

- 1 tablespoon dried lemongrass
- 2 teaspoons shredded coconut
- 2 cups boiling water

Instructions:

1. Add dried lemongrass and shredded coconut to a teapot or infuser.
2. Pour 2 cups of boiling water over the ingredients.
3. Allow the tea to steep for 6 to 8 minutes.
4. Strain and serve, enjoying the tropical flavors.

Moroccan Mint and Hibiscus Tea

Inspired by Moroccan traditions, this vibrant blend is invigorating and perfect for a refreshing moment.

Ingredients:

- 2 tablespoons dried mint leaves
- 1 tablespoon dried hibiscus flowers
- 2 cups boiling water

Instructions:

1. Place dried mint leaves and hibiscus flowers in a teapot or infuser.
2. Pour 2 cups of boiling water over them.
3. Steep for 5 to 7 minutes.
4. Strain into cups. This tea can be enjoyed hot or chilled.

Immunity-Boosting Infusions

Navigating the path of health involves a delicate balance, empowering our body's natural resilience against illness and sustaining harmony. Within this delicate interplay, herbal teas emerge as powerful allies, offering their immunity-boosting properties.

Antiviral and Antibacterial Herbs

Familiarizing yourself with these herbs is a step forward in boosting your immunity, as they are renowned for reinforcing the body's defenses. These natural powerhouses contain compounds that can help fend off infections, reduce inflammation, and enhance overall well-being. Incorporating them into your routine can be a delicious and holistic approach to health maintenance. Here are some examples of these.

- **Echinacea**: Known for its immune-boosting properties, Echinacea is a front-runner in warding off colds and other infections.
- **Ginger**: A spicy root with powerful antiviral and antibacterial properties, ginger warms the body and cleanses the system.
- **Garlic**: Though not a traditional tea ingredient, garlic's potent antibacterial and antiviral properties can be harnessed in infusions.
- **Turmeric**: With its active ingredient, curcumin, turmeric is a strong antibacterial and antiviral herb, which also lends a vibrant color to your brew.

Harnessing Herbal Teas for Immunity Boosting

Herbal teas have been a part of traditional medicine across cultures for centuries, and now contemporary research underscores their potential to enhance immune function. The bioactive compounds in herbs have been found to support the immune system in various ways, including modulating immune response and exhibiting antiviral and antibacterial properties.

A Steep in Wellness

Brewing a cup of herbal tea can be one of the simplest yet impactful routines you can adopt for bolstering your immunity. The process begins by selecting herbs known for their immune-boosting properties. Here is how you can go about it:

- **Educate Yourself**: Understand the properties of various herbs. Know which herbs have antiviral, antibacterial, and immune-modulating properties.
- **Quality Matters**: Source high-quality, organic, or wildcrafted herbs for your teas. The purity and quality of herbs significantly impact their efficacy.

- **Brew Right**: The method of brewing can also affect the potency of your tea. Ensure that you follow the recommended brewing times and temperatures to extract the maximum benefits from the herbs.

Consistent Consumption

Consistency is key when it comes to reaping the immune-boosting benefits of herbal teas. Incorporating herbal teas into your daily routine ensures a steady intake of the beneficial compounds that support your immune system.

- **Routine Brewing**: Make it a habit to brew a cup in the morning or in the evening. Find a routine that works for you and stick to it.
- **Mindful Consumption**: Enjoy the process. Sipping tea mindfully enhances the overall experience and nurtures a deeper connection to your wellness journey.

Herbal Tea Recipes

Creating immunity-boosting infusions encapsulates a beautiful blend of traditional knowledge and modern understanding. The meticulous selection of herbs, the gentle simmering, and the patient steeping all contribute towards concocting a brew that is not only pleasing to the palate but also beneficial to the body.

Echinacea Elderberry Tea

The combination of Echinacea and elderberry in a warm cup is nothing short of an immune system's delight. Both these herbs have been traditionally revered for their immune-boosting properties. The synergy of Echinacea and elderberry offers a fortified defense against common colds and other infections, making this tea a worthy companion, especially during the cold season.

Ingredients:

- 1 tablespoon dried Echinacea
- 1 tablespoon dried elderberries
- 2 cups water

Method:

1. Bring water to a rolling boil in a stainless steel or glass pot.
2. Reduce the heat, add the herbs, and let it simmer for about 15 minutes.
3. Strain the herbs into your favorite mug using a fine-mesh strainer.
4. Enjoy the blend hot, perhaps with a touch of honey if desired.

Ginger Lemon Infusion

The zing of ginger, coupled with the tang of lemon, makes for a refreshing and invigorating brew. Beyond its invigorating taste, this infusion is a powerhouse of antiviral and antibacterial properties. The synergy of Echinacea and elderberry offers a fortified defense against common colds and other infections, making this tea a worthy companion, especially during the cold season.

Ingredients:

- 1-inch fresh ginger root, sliced
- 1 lemon, sliced
- 2 cups water

Method:

1. In a pot, bring water to a boil.
2. Add the sliced ginger and allow it to simmer for about 10 minutes.

3. Turn off the heat, add the lemon slices, cover the pot, and let it steep for an additional 10 minutes.
4. Strain and pour into a cup, relishing the spicy, citrusy aroma before taking your first sip.

Turmeric Black Pepper Tea

The golden hue of turmeric blended with a hint of black pepper leads to a brew that is as pleasing visually as it is beneficial health-wise.

Ingredients:

- 1 teaspoon turmeric powder
- A pinch of black pepper
- 2 cups water

Method:

1. Bring water to a boil.
2. Stir in the turmeric powder and black pepper, allowing the blend to simmer for about 10 minutes.
3. Strain the brew into a mug, perhaps adding a touch of honey for a hint of sweetness.

Hibiscus and Cinnamon Immunity Tea

This tea blends the tart, vitamin C-rich hibiscus with sweet and warming cinnamon, creating an infusion that is not only delightful in taste but also excellent for immune support.

Ingredients:

- 2 tablespoons dried hibiscus flowers
- 1 cinnamon stick
- 2 cups water

Method:

1. Boil water in a pot.
2. Add the hibiscus flowers and cinnamon stick.
3. Simmer for 10 to 15 minutes.
4. Strain into a cup and enjoy. You can add honey for sweetness if desired.

Sage and Thyme Wellness Tea

Sage and thyme, both herbs with powerful antimicrobial properties, create a tea that is not only beneficial for throat health but also for overall immunity. This tea has a savory, earthy flavor, making it a unique choice.

Ingredients:

- 1 tablespoon dried sage leaves
- 1 teaspoon dried thyme
- 2 cups boiling water

Method:

1. Combine sage and thyme in a teapot or infuser.
2. Pour boiling water over the herbs and steep for about 10 minutes.
3. Strain and enjoy, adding honey to taste if desired.

Digestive Soothers

The rhythm of our lives often mirrors the rhythm of our digestive system. A harmonious, well-functioning digestion is the cornerstone of good health, and yet, it is a realm often disrupted by the hustle of our daily lives. Understanding the basics of the digestive system, exploring the benefits of post-meal teas, and discovering herbal teas crafted for digestive health nurtures one of the most vital systems in your body.

Digestive System Overview

The digestive system is a complex network of organs, all collaborating to convert the food we eat into energy and basic nutrients to fuel the body.

Importance

Promoting digestive system wellness is critical because this system is the foundation of your body's health. It breaks down the foods you eat into the nutrients your body needs. If your digestive system is not working efficiently, your body cannot absorb these vital nutrients properly.

A healthy digestive system also plays a crucial role in immunity. Much of the immune system is in the gastrointestinal tract. Maintaining a healthy gut flora through a balanced diet, including the regular consumption of herbal teas, is essential for supporting a robust immune response.

Additionally, a smoothly functioning digestive system helps prevent various gastrointestinal issues, such as bloating, gas, heartburn, constipation, and diarrhea. Many herbal teas contain ingredients that naturally combat these symptoms and promote gut health.

Digestion is also connected to our mood and energy levels. Issues in the digestive tract can lead to feelings of lethargy or a drop in mood. Therefore, a well-cared-for digestive system can mean not just physical comfort but also mental and emotional well-being.

Incorporating herbal teas into your diet is a simple, pleasurable way to support your digestive health. Their warmth and herbal properties work to soothe the digestive tract, reduce inflammation, and encourage a balanced digestive process.

Post-meal Tea Benefits

The ritual of post-meal tea is an age-old tradition in many cultures due to the following:

- **Aiding Digestion:** A warm cup of herbal tea can aid in the digestion process, helping to break down food more efficiently, which in turn can alleviate feelings of heaviness or bloating post meals.
- **Soothing Effect:** Herbal teas can have a soothing effect on the digestive tract, calming any inflammation or irritation and creating a conducive environment for digestion and absorption.
- **Enhancing Nutrient Absorption:** Certain herbal teas can also aid in better nutrient absorption, ensuring that your body reaps the maximum benefits from the food you consume.

Nurturing Digestive Wellness with Herbal Teas

Each herb selected for these recipes holds a unique signature of benefits tailored toward nurturing digestive wellness. The following herbal tea recipes are curated keeping in mind the gentle caress that the digestive system often longs for amidst the hustle of your daily life.

Lemon Balm Tea

Lemon Balm, with its mild lemon scent, is known for its calming effects on the digestive system, helping to ease gas and bloating.

Ingredients:

- 2 tablespoons dried lemon balm leaves
- 2 cups water

Method:

1. Bring water to a boil in a stainless steel or glass pot.
2. Add lemon balm leaves, cover the pot, and let it steep for about 10 minutes.
3. Strain the leaves and pour the tea into a cup.
4. Enjoy the mild, lemony flavor of this soothing tea.

Dandelion Root Tea

Dandelion Root is a powerhouse of digestive support, aiding in liver detoxification and promoting healthy digestion.

Ingredients:

- 2 tablespoons dried dandelion root
- 2 cups water

Method:

1. Boil water and remove from heat.
2. Add dandelion root, cover, and let it steep for about 10 minutes.
3. Strain the root and relish the earthy flavor of dandelion.

Caraway Seed Tea

Caraway Seeds have a long tradition of being used to alleviate gas, bloating, and digestive spasms.

Ingredients:

- 1 tablespoon caraway seeds
- 2 cups water

Method:

1. Lightly crush the caraway seeds in a mortar to release their oils.
2. Bring water to a boil, add the crushed caraway seeds, reduce heat, and let it simmer for about 10 minutes.
3. Strain the seeds and savor the warm, sweet, and slightly peppery flavor of caraway.

Licorice Root Tea

Licorice Root is a sweet, slightly spicy herb known for soothing the digestive tract and supporting gastric health.

Ingredients:

- 1 tablespoon licorice root, cut and sifted
- 2 cups water

Method:

1. Bring water to a boil.
2. Add licorice root, cover, and let it simmer on low heat for about 10 minutes.
3. Strain the root and enjoy the sweet, slightly spicy flavor of licorice.

Chapter 6

Cultivating a Herbal Tea Garden

Growing your own herbal tea garden can be an extremely rewarding endeavor. It allows you to connect with nature while producing your own selection of aromatic and therapeutic teas. In this chapter, you will be guided through the initial planning stages of creating a thriving tea garden. Key steps like choosing the ideal location, designing the layout, selecting herbs suited to your climate, preparing the soil, employing proper planting techniques, and maintaining and harvesting your tea garden will be covered. You will gain invaluable insights into transforming a bare patch of land into a flourishing sanctuary brimming with your personally cultivated herbs for crafting flavorful herbal infusions. This chapter illuminates the foundational practices and guiding principles behind establishing and nurturing a productive tea garden that will bring you joy for seasons to come.

Planning Your Tea Garden

Creating a tea garden is an exciting venture. It allows you to immerse in nature while cultivating your personal selection of herbal teas right in your backyard. Below are the fundamental steps in ensuring that your herbal tea garden flourishes.

Selecting a Site

Creating a beautiful and productive tea garden starts with picking the right spot. It is all about finding that perfect piece of land where your tea plants will thrive. In this part of the guide, you'll dive into the key elements—like the amount of sun, the type of soil, and how easy it is to get to—that you need to consider picking the best place for your tea garden. When you choose wisely, you give your tea herbs the best chance to grow strong and healthy, which means they will taste better and be packed with more goodness for your brews.

Sunlight

Sunlight is the lifeblood of plants. Herbs bask in the glory of the sun, and the site you select should be generously bathed in sunlight for a good part of the day. Generally, a spot that basks in at least 6 to 8 hours of sunlight daily is the sweet spot. You would do well to observe the sunlight pattern in your yard over a few days to pinpoint the spot that meets this golden criterion. Consider using a sun calculator or a solar pathfinder to gauge the sun exposure of potential garden sites accurately. The more precise you are in ensuring adequate sunlight, the lusher and more vibrant your tea garden will be.

Soil Quality

The soil is more than just the dirt beneath our feet; it is the nurturing cradle that feeds the roots of your herbs. High-quality soil is rich in essential nutrients and has a friendly pH level for your plants. Before you plunge into planting, test the soil for its pH level and nutrient content. Most herbs cozy up to slightly acidic to neutral soil with a pH level hovering around 6.0 to 7.0. If the soil at your chosen site does not make the cut, do not be disheartened.

Amending the soil with organic matter or other soil amendments can tip the pH scale in your favor. Investing time in priming the soil is like investing in a good mattress; it is the comforting support your herbs need to grow.

Accessibility

A garden that is easily accessible is a garden that is easy to care for. As you mull over potential sites, lean towards spots that are a stone's throw away from your house or a water source. This proximity will make the daily chores of watering, harvesting, and maintenance less of a slog and more of a joyful jaunt. Moreover, an accessible garden beckons you to spend time in it, transforming the routine task of watering into a meditative morning ritual.

In the long run, the ease of accessibility to your garden will mean fewer skipped watering days, prompt pest control, and timely harvesting, all of which contribute to a thriving tea garden. The simple act of selecting an accessible site can significantly streamline your gardening routine, making the cultivation of your herbal teas a more enjoyable and less cumbersome endeavor.

Designing the Layout

Designing the layout of your tea garden is where creativity intertwines with practicality. This phase allows you to sketch a blueprint of your garden's aesthetics while ensuring it remains a functional space for cultivation. The layout is the canvas where your gardening skills and aesthetic sense will paint a living picture. As you design, remember that a well-thought-out layout is the cornerstone of a garden that is both beautiful and easy to maintain.

Pathways and Beds

The heartbeat of a well-designed garden is in its pathways and beds. Clear, unobstructed pathways are your allies in maintaining a garden that is easy to navigate. When laying out the pathways, envision how you will move through the garden for watering, weeding, and harvesting. A width of at least 2 feet for the pathways is a good rule of thumb to ensure comfortable access.

When it comes to beds, their design should cater to the growth habits of your chosen herbs. Arrange the beds such that taller herbs like lemon balm or fennel do not cast a shadow over sun-loving shorter herbs like thyme or oregano. A popular and practical approach is to plant herbs in a tiered fashion or in raised beds, which not only ensures adequate sunlight for all plants but also creates a dynamic visual effect.

Aesthetic Appeal

A garden is more than a cultivation ground; it is a space of visual and sensory delight. The aesthetics of your garden layout play a pivotal role in making your garden a pleasant sanctuary. Incorporate curves rather than rigid lines to add a soft, natural flow to the layout. Use a mix of colors, textures, and heights to create a visually engaging space. For instance, the delicate purple blooms of lavender can create a stunning contrast next to the bright green foliage of mint.

Also, consider adding a focal point like a birdbath, a small fountain, or a charming garden bench. These elements draw the eye and offer a place of rest, adding a touch of whimsy to your tea garden. Moreover, the use of repeating color schemes or plant varieties in different parts of the garden can bring a sense of cohesiveness and harmony.

Choosing Your Herbs

A delightful tea garden largely hinges on the herbs you choose to plant. Your selection of herbs reflects your taste, the teas you fancy, and the local growing conditions. The following is the process of choosing herbs that resonate with your taste buds and are well-poised to thrive in the conditions your garden offers.

Research

Doing a bit of research before you decide on the herbs is a wise step. Familiarize yourself with various herbs, understanding their growth habits, height, spread, and the conditions they thrive in. Each herb comes with its own palette of flavors and medicinal benefits. For instance, mint is invigorating and aids digestion, chamomile is calming and helps with sleep, while lavender is soothing and has antiseptic properties.

Explore the teas you enjoy and investigate the herbs that are used in them. Books on herbal teas, gardening blogs, and local nurseries can be treasure troves of information. You might also consider joining a local gardening club or online forums to glean insights from other tea garden enthusiasts.

Climate and Soil

The temperament of your local climate and the character of your soil are significant determinants in the success of your herb garden. Some herbs are sun-worshippers, while others thrive in cool, shaded spots. Similarly, while most herbs prefer well-draining soil, some thrive in moist conditions.

Look for herbs that are well-suited to your area's hardiness zone. Local nurseries are excellent sources for plants adapted to your region, and the staff can provide invaluable advice. It is also beneficial to observe successful gardens in your area and note the herbs that seem to thrive.

When it comes to soil, a simple soil test can reveal its pH and nutrient levels. Match your herb choices to the soil conditions, or be prepared to amend the soil to meet the needs of the herbs you wish to grow.

Experimentation

Do not shy away from a little experimentation. Every garden is a learning ground, and sometimes, a herb may surprise you by thriving in unexpected conditions. Start with a few herbs, and as you gain confidence, expand your garden by introducing new herbs one season at a time.

In conclusion, the choice of herbs is a personal journey molded by your preferences and the unique conditions of your garden. With a dash of research, a sprinkle of local knowledge, and a spoonful of experimentation, you will be well on your way to cultivating a tea garden that is brimming with flavor and personal satisfaction. Through this thoughtful selection process, your tea garden will not only be a source of delightful teas but also a haven for learning and discovery in the beautiful world of herbs.

Preparing and Planting

The act of preparing and planting is a transformative journey where a barren plot morphs into a thriving tea garden. It is in this phase that your carefully selected herbs meet the nurturing earth, setting the stage for a bountiful harvest.

Soil Preparation

Soil is the cradle that supports the life of your garden. Preparing the soil is like laying a solid foundation for a house. A well-prepared soil ensures that your herbs have the right environment to grow healthy, which in turn affects the quality, flavor, and medicinal properties of your herbal teas.

Testing and Amending Soil

Initiate your soil preparation by conducting a soil test to determine its pH and nutrient levels. Herbs generally favor a pH range of 6.0 to 7.0. Should your soil be too acidic or alkaline, amendments like lime or sulfur can help balance the pH. Incorporating organic matter such as compost or well-rotted manure will enrich the soil with vital nutrients and improve its texture.

Tilling and Loosening Soil

Tilling the soil to a depth of 12 to 15 inches helps to loosen compacted earth, making it easier for roots to spread and access water and nutrients. It is also a good time to weed out any unwanted plants that could compete with your herbs for resources.

Planting Techniques

Planting is the moment when your chosen herbs finally find their home in your garden. The method you employ in planting can significantly impact the growth and yield of your herbs. Correct planting techniques ensure that your herbs are well-positioned to grow vigorously, promising a bountiful harvest for your herbal tea concoctions.

Seed Starting vs Transplants

You have the choice of starting your herbs from seeds or transplanting young plants. Seeds are cost-effective and offer a wider variety, while transplants provide a head start in the growing season.

Planting Depth and Spacing

Adhere to the recommended planting depth and spacing for each herb type. Overcrowding can lead to inadequate sunlight and airflow, which could foster the growth of pests and diseases.

Watering and Fertilization

Water and nutrients are the lifeblood of your garden.

Watering Guidelines

Proper watering and fertilization ensure that your herbs are nourished and hydrated, which directly influences the potency and flavor of your herbal teas. Herbs prefer deep, infrequent watering to shallow, frequent watering. Early morning is the ideal time to water as it allows the plants to absorb the moisture before the sun evaporates it.

Fertilization Essentials

While herbs are generally low-feeders, a balanced, slow-release organic fertilizer can be beneficial. Always adhere to the recommended dosage to prevent over-fertilization, which can be detrimental to your plants.

Maintenance and Harvesting

Maintaining and harvesting your tea garden is akin to nurturing a narrative that began with a mere seed. It is where your diligence manifests into lush, aromatic herbs ready to be plucked.

Pest and Weed Management

An uninvited ensemble of pests and weeds can often disrupt the peaceful cultivation of your garden. Here is how you can keep your herbal retreat healthy and bountiful, warding off pests and weeds effectively and sustainably.

Integrated Pest Management (IPM):

Integrated Pest Management (IPM) is your garden's proactive strategy for defense. Instead of waiting for problems to escalate, you are keeping a vigilant eye out and stepping in at the first sign of trouble. Regular checks are key—they are your early warning system to spot pests before they become a bigger issue.

When you do notice unwanted visitors, it is important to pinpoint exactly what kind of pest you are dealing with. Once identified, choose the control method that poses the least risk to the environment, your plants, and beneficial insects. For example, if aphids are the culprits, consider introducing ladybugs to your garden. They are nature's pest control agents and will happily dine on the aphids, managing the problem in an eco-conscious way.

Unwanted Weeds

Imagine your garden as an exclusive event, and weeds are those party crashers nobody invited. To keep these gatecrashers out, laying down mulch is like hiring a security guard for the soil. Mulch covers the ground, keeping weed seeds in the dark and stopping them from ever sprouting. If some weeds manage to sneak in, you will want to remove them completely—roots and all—by hand-pulling or using a hoe to slice them off at the ground.

Handy Tips for a Weed-Free Garden:

- Integrate natural pest deterrents into your garden by planting herbs like lavender and rosemary, which are known to send pests packing.
- Apply a generous blanket of mulch around your plants. This not only keeps the weeds down but also helps your soil keep cool and stay hydrated.

Pruning and Mulching

Pruning and mulching are the beauty and health regimen for your garden.

Pruning Techniques

Pruning is like giving your herbs a rejuvenating spa day. When you prune, you are removing parts of the plants that are overgrown or unnecessary, which stimulates fresh growth and helps the plant focus its energy on producing what you want most: healthy leaves and stems.

Some pruning techniques and tips:

- Start by cutting back any branches or stems that seem overgrown, are crossing each other, or look dead or diseased. Doing so opens up the plant, improving air circulation and light exposure to the center.
- When pruning herbs like basil, make your cuts just above a set of growing leaves. This will encourage the plant to branch out from that point, leading to a fuller, bushier shape.

- Regularly snip off the tips of your herbs. This not only helps maintain their shape but also boosts leaf production.
- If you see any flowers developing, pinch them off, especially in herbs like basil and oregano. Flowering can cause the plant to put more energy into flower production rather than leaf growth, which can alter the flavor of your herbs.
- Use clean, sharp pruning shears for a clean cut, which is healthier for the plant and helps prevent disease.
- Do not be too zealous with your pruning; always leave a good amount of foliage so the plant can continue to photosynthesize and grow.
- The best time to prune is in the morning when the plants are well-hydrated and the essential oils are concentrated in the leaves, which is especially beneficial if you plan to use the pruned herbs for cooking or teas.

Mulching

Think of mulch as a cozy blanket for your garden beds—it does so much more than just making the garden look neat and tidy. This protective layer works wonders by keeping the soil temperature regulated, locking in moisture, and warding off those pesky weeds that you do not want competing with your herbs. Plus, when you use organic materials like straw or bark chips, they gradually break down and contribute to the soil's fertility.

Some mulching tips to help your garden flourish:

- Always opt for sharp, clean tools when you are cutting back plants or pruning. This ensures you get nice, clean cuts that heal quickly, and it helps to prevent any disease from sneaking into the fresh cuts.
- When you are spreading mulch, aim for a layer that is about 2 to 3 inches thick. This is the sweet spot that offers

enough coverage to reap all the benefits without smothering your plants.

- Be mindful to leave a buffer zone between the mulch and the stems of your plants. A few inches should do the trick. This space is crucial because it prevents excess moisture from accumulating around the stems, which could lead to rot and disease.
- Remember to replenish the mulch as needed, especially as the organic materials begin to break down and integrate with the soil.

Harvesting Your Herbs

Harvesting marks the rewarding conclusion to your garden's cycle of growth, a time when you gather the fruits of your labor. The following are the best practices to ensure you capture the full flavor and potency of your herbs at the very peak of their readiness.

Optimal Timing

To catch your herbs at their absolute best, aim for the early morning hours, right after the dew has lifted. This is when your herbs are most vibrant, brimming with hydration, and the essential oils that give them their flavor and aroma are at their most concentrated.

The Art of Harvesting

Approach harvesting with the finesse of an artist. Arm yourself with a pair of sharp scissors or pruners to cleanly cut the herbs, as pulling or tearing the stems can harm the plant. For varieties like mint and basil that respond well to regular cutting, make your snips right above a leaf pair. This precise technique encourages a more compact, bushier plant.

Preparing Harvested Herbs for Teas

Once the diligent process of growing and harvesting is complete, the next captivating chapter in the narrative of your tea garden unfolds, preparing the harvested herbs for teas.

Washing and Handling Techniques

The initial encounter with your harvested herbs sets the tone for the quality of tea that will eventually grace your cup. How you handle your herbs post-harvest is a determinant of the quality and potency of your teas. A gentle approach preserves the innate essence of the herbs, promising a superior tea experience.

- **Gentle Washing:** A gentle bath is the first gift to your harvested herbs. Lukewarm water is your best companion in this task. Delicately swish the herbs to dislodge any dirt or unwelcome insect travelers. It is a ritual of purity, preparing the herbs for their journey ahead.
- **Considerate Handling:** Treat your herbs with the tenderness they deserve. Avoid crushing or bruising the leaves as this could lead to loss of essential oils, which are the heart of the flavor and aroma of your teas.

Drying Herbs

Drying is a delicate process that bids farewell to the moisture in your herbs while preserving their flavor, color, and medicinal properties.

Air-Drying

Air-drying is like allowing nature to take its course. This method is gentle on the herbs, preserving their essence.

Procedure:

1. Start by tying small bunches of herbs together at the stem.
2. Hang them upside down in a warm, dry, and well-ventilated area away from direct sunlight, which could rob them of their vibrant color and potent flavors.
3. Make sure the location is clean and free from dust or any other contaminants.
4. Leave them to dry naturally. This could take anywhere from a week to several, depending on the moisture content in the herbs and the humidity in the air.
5. Once dry, the leaves should crumble easily between your fingers. Store them in airtight containers away from light and heat.

Tip: *Label your bunches with the name and date of drying to keep track, especially when drying multiple herb varieties.*

Dehydrator Drying

When time is of the essence, a dehydrator is your go-to companion. It is a controlled, faster method of drying herbs.

Procedure:

1. Pick the leaves from the stems and spread them out in a single layer on the dehydrator trays.
2. Set the temperature as per the manufacturer's instructions, generally between 95 to 115 °F.
3. The drying time can vary from 1 to 4 hours depending on the type and moisture content of the herbs.
4. Check the herbs periodically. Once they are dry and crumble easily, they are ready to be stored.

Tip: *Ensure the herbs are not overlapping or piled on top of each other, as this could lead to uneven drying.*

Freezing Herbs

Freezing is your gateway to preserving the garden-fresh quality of your herbs long after they have been harvested. It is a way to capture the essence of summer in your cup, even in the heart of winter. The preserved freshness accentuates the flavor and therapeutic benefits of your teas, making each sip a journey back to the verdant lushness of your garden.

Flash Freezing

This quick-freeze technique involves a rapid cooldown, which helps lock in the vibrant colors, essential oils, and all the aromatic goodness of your herbs as if they have just been picked from the garden.

Procedure:

1. Begin by gently washing your harvested herbs and patting them dry thoroughly with a clean towel.
2. Spread the herbs out on a baking tray in a single layer. It is important they do not overlap to ensure even freezing.
3. Place the tray in the freezer for about 1 to 2 hours or until the herbs are frozen solid.
4. Once frozen, quickly transfer the herbs into airtight containers or resealable freezer bags. Label them with the name of the herb and the date of freezing.
5. Return them to the freezer promptly to prevent them from thawing.

Tip: *For herbs with tender leaves like mint or basil, you could also chop them finely, place them in ice cube trays, fill them with water, and freeze them. These herb ice cubes can be thrown directly into the hot water when you are ready to brew your tea.*

Chapter 7

Blending Your Own Teas

Discover the art of crafting your customized herbal tea blends in this chapter. Learn the essence and benefits of blending, from being able to create a tea that caters to your taste preferences to making blends that provide specific health benefits. Fundamental blending principles are covered to help you build a solid foundation, including understanding flavor profiles, using quality ingredients, and practicing proper storage.

The Basics of Blending

Blending is an art that allows you to create a personalized tea experience by combining different herbs, flavors, and aromas. In the context of herbal teas, blending allows you to mix various herbs, each with its unique flavor profile and health benefits, to create a cup that is beneficial to your health.

Benefits of Blending

Blending your own teas provides an avenue to explore, experiment, and create something uniquely yours. It allows you to tailor your tea blends according to your taste preferences, health needs, or even the mood you are in. Furthermore, blending can elevate the sensory experience of tea drinking, making it more enjoyable and therapeutic. For instance, blending peppermint with rooibos can provide a refreshing yet earthy flavor, ideal for a morning pick-me-up.

Fundamental Principles of Blending

Understanding some basic principles can set you on the right path to blending success. Here are a few guidelines:

- **Balance**: Aim for a balanced blend where no single ingredient overpowers the others. Balance in flavor, aroma, and therapeutic benefits is key to a good blend.
- **Harmony**: Ensure the ingredients complement each other. They should work together to create a harmonious blend rather than clashing or competing.
- **Quality**: Use high-quality, fresh ingredients to ensure the best results. The quality of ingredients significantly impacts the final blend.
- **Proportions**: Start with a basic ratio and adjust according to taste. For example, a simple blend might start with equal parts of each herb, and adjustments can be made from there.
- **Simplicity**: Especially for beginners, starting with a few ingredients can help you understand how different herbs interact before moving on to more complex blends.

Safety Considerations

The safety of your blends is as important as the taste and therapeutic benefits they offer. Here are some key points to consider:

- **Knowledge of Ingredients**: It is essential to have a basic understanding of the herbs you are using, including their health benefits, potential side effects, and interactions with other herbs or medications. For instance, while St. John's Wort is popular for its potential to alleviate mild depression, it can interact negatively with certain medications.

- **Check for Allergy and Sensitivity:** Before experimenting with new herbs, ensure you or the individuals who will be consuming the blend do not have any allergies or sensitivities to the ingredients. Conducting a small patch test or consulting with a healthcare professional can be prudent steps.
- **Cleanliness**: Ensure that your blending area, utensils, and containers are clean to prevent contamination. It is also advisable to wash your hands thoroughly before handling herbs and other blending materials.
- **Quality Assurance**: Always use fresh, high-quality herbs from reputable sources to ensure the safety and effectiveness of your blends. It is advisable to avoid using old or expired herbs as they can be ineffective or potentially harmful.
- **Proper Storage**: Store your herbal blends in a cool, dry place away from direct sunlight to maintain their potency and prevent spoilage. Utilizing airtight containers can also help in preserving the freshness and efficacy of your blends.
- **Consultation with Healthcare Professionals**: If you are pregnant, nursing, have underlying health conditions, or are on medication, it is wise to consult with a healthcare professional before experimenting with herbal blends.
- **Labeling**: Properly label your blends with the ingredients and the date of blending. This practice is especially helpful if you create various blends and helps ensure you are consuming them while they are still fresh and effective.

Herbal Tea Blend Ideas

The world of herbal teas is a vast and colorful one, brimming with a variety of flavors, aromas, and health benefits. Each category offers a unique approach to blending, whether it is adhering to age-old combinations, aligning with the rhythm of the seasons, or targeting specific health concerns. As you explore these ideas, you will find inspiration to craft your own signature blends and discover the endless possibilities that the art of blending unfolds.

Classic Blend Ideas

These classic blends are easy to prepare and offer a delightful array of flavors. Each blend has a timeless appeal that makes them a cherished choice across various cultures and palates. They serve as a reminder of the simplicity and the holistic approach of traditional tea blending.

Earl Grey-Lavender Blend

The Earl Grey-Lavender blend is a fragrant fusion that carries the bold, citrusy notes of Earl Grey tea with the soft, calming aroma of lavender. This blend is perfect for those afternoons when you seek relaxation with a touch of invigoration. The delicate lavender not only complements the robust Earl Grey but adds a layer of tranquility to the blend.

Ingredients:

- 3 tablespoons of Earl Grey tea leaves
- 1 tablespoon of dried lavender buds

Instructions:

1. Mix the Earl Grey tea leaves and dried lavender buds in a clean, dry bowl.
2. Transfer the mixture to a tea infuser or tea bag.
3. Boil water to 200 °F (93 °C) and pour it over the tea mixture.
4. Steep it for 3 to 5 minutes, depending on your taste preference.

5. Remove the infuser or tea bag, pour it into a cup, and enjoy the aromatic elegance.

Lemon-Ginger Blend

The Lemon-Ginger Blend is a zesty concoction that combines the refreshing citrus notes of lemon with the spicy, invigorating kick of ginger. It is an excellent blend for early mornings or as a revitalizing brew during a mid-day slump. The lemon adds a refreshing clarity, while the ginger provides a warm, stimulating feel, making this blend a well-balanced energizer.

Ingredients:

- 2 tablespoons of dried lemon peel or dried lemon verbena leaves
- 1 tablespoon of fresh ginger, thinly sliced

Instructions:

1. Mix the dried lemon peel or lemon verbena leaves and fresh ginger slices in a bowl.
2. Place the mixture in a tea infuser or tea bag.
3. Boil water to 212 °F (100 °C), then pour it over the tea mixture.
4. Steep the leaves and adjust the time for the desired flavor intensity.
5. Remove the infuser or tea bag, pour into a cup, and relish the citrus-spice infusion.

Apple-Cinnamon Blend

The Apple-Cinnamon Blend is a comforting, cozy blend that encapsulates the essence of a warm, homey kitchen. The sweet, tart notes of dried apple pieces blend harmoniously with the spicy warmth of cinnamon, creating a cup that is both soothing and stimulating. It is a perfect blend to enjoy during autumn, although its comforting vibes make it a cherished choice year-round.

Ingredients:

- 2 tablespoons of dried apple pieces
- 1 cinnamon stick, broken into pieces

Instructions:

1. Mix the dried apple pieces and cinnamon stick pieces in a bowl.
2. Transfer the mixture to a tea infuser or tea bag.
3. Boil water to 212 °F (100 °C), then pour it over the tea mixture.
4. Let it steep for 5 to 7 minutes, depending on your taste preference.
5. Remove the infuser or tea bag, pour into a cup, and bask in the cozy, comforting flavors.

Seasonal Blend Ideas

Aligning your tea blends with the changing seasons can be a delightful way to connect with nature's rhythm. Seasonal blends reflect the essence of each season, providing what the body craves and needs during that time.

Spring Blend

The spring blend is a light, floral concoction that mirrors the fresh, blooming essence of spring. It is a blend that invites you to shake off the winter chills and embrace the budding warmth of a new season.

Ingredients:

- 2 tablespoons of dried lavender buds
- 2 tablespoons of dried rose petals
- 2 tablespoons of dried chamomile flowers

Instructions:

1. In a bowl, gently mix the lavender buds, rose petals, and chamomile flowers.
2. Place the mixture in a tea infuser or tea bag.
3. Boil water to 212 °F (100 °C), then pour it over the tea blend.
4. Allow it to steep for 5 to 7 minutes, adjusting the time to achieve your desired flavor intensity.
5. Remove the infuser or tea bag, pour into a cup, and enjoy the rejuvenating floral notes of spring.

Summer Blend

The Summer blend is a cooling, refreshing mixture designed to provide a soothing retreat from the scorching summer heat. It is your perfect companion on a warm sunny day, promising a refreshing breeze with every sip.

Ingredients:

- 2 tablespoons of dried peppermint leaves
- 2 tablespoons of dried lemon balm leaves
- 2 tablespoons of dried hibiscus flowers

Instructions:

1. Combine the dried peppermint, lemon balm, and hibiscus flowers in a bowl and mix well.

2. Transfer the mixture to a tea infuser or tea bag.
3. Boil water to 212 °F (100 °C), then pour it over the tea blend.
4. Let it steep for 5 to 7 minutes, depending on your taste preference.
5. Remove the infuser or tea bag, pour into a cup, and enjoy the cooling, revitalizing sip of summer.

Autumn Blend

The Autumn blend is a warm, spicy concoction that encapsulates the cozy, comforting vibe of fall. It is a blend that invites you to wrap yourself in a blanket, watch the leaves fall, and enjoy the crisp autumn air.

Ingredients:

- 1 cinnamon stick, broken into pieces
- 1 tablespoon of fresh ginger, thinly sliced
- 1 tablespoon of dried clove buds

Instructions:

1. Mix the cinnamon stick pieces, ginger slices, and clove buds in a bowl.
2. Place the mixture in a tea infuser or tea bag.
3. Boil water to 212 °F (100 °C), then pour it over the tea blend.
4. Allow it to steep for 5 to 7 minutes, adjusting the time for the desired flavor intensity.
5. Remove the infuser or tea bag, pour into a cup, and relish the warm, spicy notes of autumn.

Winter Blend

The Winter Blend is a hearty, robust mixture aimed at supporting immune health during the cold, harsh winter months. It is a blend that promises to keep you warm and bolstered against the winter chill.

Ingredients:

- 2 tablespoons of dried echinacea flowers
- 2 tablespoons of dried elderberries
- 1 tablespoon of fresh ginger, thinly sliced

Instructions:

1. In a bowl, mix the echinacea flowers, elderberries, and ginger slices.
2. Transfer the blend to a tea infuser or tea bag.
3. Boil water to 212 °F (100 °C), then pour it over the tea blend.
4. Let it steep for 5 to 7 minutes, depending on your taste preference.
5. Remove the infuser or tea bag, pour into a cup, and savor the hearty, immune-supporting warmth of winter.

Troubleshooting Blends

The craft of creating your personal tea blends is a canvas of creativity and exploration, rich with the excitement of combining flavors and the joy of discovery. But as with any art, you may encounter a few bumps along the way. It is all part of the process.

Getting comfortable with the troubleshooting process is invaluable—it sharpens your intuition for flavors and brings you closer to that perfect blend that feels like it has been made just for you.

Common Blending Issues

One of the initial steps toward mastering the art of blending is identifying common issues that might arise. Recognizing these challenges early can save you time and resources.

Overpowering Flavors

It is a common scenario where a potent herb overshadows the other ingredients, making the blend taste one-dimensional. For instance, a hint of peppermint is refreshing, but when overpowering, it can mask the gentle calmness of chamomile in the blend. This is where the art of balancing kicks in. Each herb comes with its unique flavor profile; understanding and respecting their individual strengths and weaknesses helps in creating a harmonious blend.

Inconsistent Taste

Blending is a meticulous art. A slight alteration in ingredient ratios can lead to a different taste profile. Imagine sipping your favorite chamomile-lavender blend one evening and finding it soothing, but the next evening, it tastes more lavender-forward, disrupting the calmness you were expecting. Consistency in ingredient ratios is key to ensuring that every cup of tea offers the comforting experience you desire. Moreover, it is not just about the taste; inconsistent ratios can also affect the therapeutic benefits associated with the blend.

Lack of Flavor

Finding your meticulously crafted rose-lemongrass blend tasting bland can be disheartening. The lack of flavor can be due to various factors like the age or quality of the herbs. Fresh, high-quality herbs are the backbone of a flavorful, aromatic blend. The older the herb, the more likely it is to lose its flavor and potency. Storing herbs properly further plays a role in maintaining their flavors.

The lack of flavor could also point towards a need for a more complex or diversified blend. Perhaps introducing a new herb or adjusting the ratios could add that missing zing to your blend.

Adjusting Ratios and Ingredients

Understanding the essence of each ingredient and its impact on the blend is necessary. Here is how you can adjust ratios and ingredients for a balanced blend.

Identify Dominant and Subtle Ingredients

Recognize the strength of each ingredient, as dominant herbs like ginger can easily overpower subtle ones like green tea. The aim should always be to achieve a harmonious balance. For instance, if ginger's robust flavor is overshadowing the delicate notes of green tea, reducing its quantity or even substituting it with a milder spice like cinnamon might solve the issue.

Experiment with Ratios

When it comes to adjusting ratios, it is wise to start with small changes. A slight tweak can significantly alter the flavor profile of a blend. It is recommended to make incremental adjustments, altering the quantity of one ingredient at a time to clearly understand its impact. For example, if the lavender in your lavender-chamomile blend is too overpowering, reducing it by a small amount initially, say a quarter or half teaspoon, could help in achieving the desired balance.

Substitute or Add Ingredients

The freshness and quality of your ingredients significantly affect the flavor and aroma of your blend. Stale or old herbs can result in a lackluster blend. Additionally, the introduction of complementary ingredients can elevate the flavor and aroma of your blend. For instance, if your rose and hibiscus blend is tasting flat, a hint of citrus, like a lemon peel, or a touch of mint could brighten up the flavors. Do not hesitate to experiment with new ingredients; sometimes, a dash of an unexpected herb can transform your blend. Adding a hint of vanilla to a classic chai blend could introduce a sweet, creamy undertone, adding a layer of complexity and richness.

Adjusting for Taste and Aroma

Individual taste and aroma preferences play a significant role in blending. It is essential to brew a small amount of your blend, taste it, and inhale its aroma to evaluate its flavor and fragrance profile. *Is it too bitter, too mild, too sweet, or just right? Similarly, is the aroma pleasing, too strong, or not fragrant enough?* Based on your observations, you may need to make adjustments. This might mean enhancing the presence of one ingredient, lessening the dominance of another, or introducing a new ingredient to add a desired flavor or aroma. For instance, if your mint and lemon balm blend is too minty, you might consider reducing the mint or adding more lemon balm until you achieve your desired flavor balance.

Taste Testing and Adjusting

Taste testing is the key to mastering your blends. It allows you to understand the harmony between ingredients and make necessary adjustments.

Initial Taste Testing

The first sip of your blend is like a handshake, introducing the medley of flavors it harbors. When you taste your blend initially, do it with a clear mind and a clean palate. Take a moment to taste not just with your taste buds but with your senses. Feel the warmth, taste the sweetness, bitterness, or spiciness, and smell the aroma. Initial impressions are crucial as they provide a clear picture of where your blend stands.

Tip: *Avoid tasting when you have a cold or when your taste buds are influenced by other strong flavors. The objective is to get an accurate taste profile.*

Adjust and Retest

Once you have tasted and noted down your observations, it is time to roll up your sleeves and adjust. Be patient and make one adjustment at a time; this way, you will know exactly what worked and what did not.

Tip: *It is a good practice to adjust in small increments. If a flavor is too strong, reduce it little by little, or if it is too weak, strengthen it gradually.*

Record Your Observations

Keeping a blending journal can be a game-changer. It is where you can jot down every little detail of your blending process, from the types and ratios of herbs to your taste, observations, and adjustments made. It is your personal encyclopedia that will grow with every blend. Be detailed in your observations. Note down the date, the exact measurements, the source of your ingredients, and even the weather if you like. All these details provide valuable insights over time.

Continuous Learning

Every taste test and adjustment is a step towards honing your blending skills. The more you taste and adjust, the more you understand the behavior and characteristics of different herbs and how they interact with each other. Do not stop at your first success. Continue experimenting, tasting, and adjusting. Try introducing a new herb to your successful blend and see how it transforms.

Chapter 8

Herbal Tea Remedies

Herbal teas have long been valued for their healing properties and comforting warmth. In the following chapter, you will explore the world of herbal tea remedies and their potential benefits for various ailments. Learn how herbal teas can provide natural relief for common health complaints in a gentle, holistic manner. Discover too how to craft custom tea blends to find soothing solutions tailored to your needs. From settling an upset stomach to alleviating insomnia, herbal teas can be simple, accessible allies for wellness.

Remedies for Common Ailments

In the comfort of your home, you often search for remedies that are natural, readily available, and without the need for a trip to the doctor for minor ailments. In this search, herbal teas emerge as a haven of potential benefits.

Benefits of Treating Ailments Naturally

In a world where quick fixes and fast relief are often sought after, it is worth exploring the road less traveled — the path of natural remedies like herbal teas. *Why opt for these plant-based brews over the standard pill?* The answer lies not just in what they alleviate but in how they heal. Here are some of the notable benefits they offer.

The Gentle Approach

Herbal teas work with a subtlety that is often underestimated. Unlike many medications that charge through your system like a bull in a Chinese shop, herbal remedies offer a gentler approach. They coax your body back to health rather than pushing it, encouraging a natural healing process without overwhelming it.

Holistic Healing

Consider the difference between patching up a leak and fixing the plumbing. Conventional medicines tend to target the symptoms — they patch up the leak. Herbal teas, on the other hand, aim to address the root cause of the ailment. This holistic perspective not only treats the symptoms but also nurtures the overall well-being of the body, fostering a balance that may prevent future issues.

Supporting the Body's Defenses

Your body has a remarkable ability to heal itself, and natural remedies can be the perfect support crew in this process. Rather than taking over the job, herbs like echinacea, for instance, support the immune system, giving it a nudge to work more effectively. This way, you are not just fighting off today's discomfort but strengthening your defenses for tomorrow.

Fewer Side Effects

Often, the conventional route of treatment comes with a package of side effects — some of which might require another round of medication to manage. Herbal teas play a different tune. They are usually free from the harsh side effects that accompany many prescription drugs. This means you can sip your way to better health without bracing for an unwanted aftermath.

Sustainable and Accessible Wellness

Let us not forget the ease of integrating herbal teas into your daily routine. While some medications require a prescription and come with a high price tag, herbal teas are readily available and can be a cost-effective part of your wellness regimen. This accessibility makes it a sustainable choice for ongoing health management.

Empowerment in Your Hands

Lastly, there is something empowering about taking charge of your health with remedies that have been used for centuries. Learning to select and blend herbs for a tea that targets your specific ailment can be incredibly satisfying. It puts the power back in your hands, or in this case, in your teacup.

Addressing Everyday Ailments with Herbal Teas

In the pursuit of relief from everyday health complaints, you need not look further than your tea cupboard. Herbal teas, with their rich array of properties, stand ready to ease your discomfort, offering natural remedies for many common symptoms, some of which are listed below.

Combatting the Common Cold

A sniffle here, a cough there, and before you know it, you are down with the common cold. A traditional tea remedy often includes peppermint, hailed for its menthol content, which eases breathing. Elderflower acts as a gentle immune booster and decongestant. Add a slice of ginger for its anti-inflammatory properties, and you have a trifecta of ingredients poised to help lessen the grip of cold symptoms.

Traditional Cold Relief Tea

Here is a recipe you could follow for making traditional cold relief tea.

Ingredients:

- 1 tbsp Echinacea
- 1 tbsp Elderberry
- 1 tbsp Peppermint leaves
- Honey *(to taste)*
- 1 tsp Lemon juice

Instructions:

1. Steep the echinacea, elderberry, and peppermint leaves in boiling water for 10 minutes.
2. Strain and add honey and lemon juice to taste.

Settling an Upset Stomach

Nausea, indigestion, and general stomach upset can arise from a variety of causes, but relief may be just a cup of tea away. Ginger, with its stomach-soothing properties, is a go-to herb that can help settle the digestive tract. Peppermint tea is another favorite that relaxes the digestive system and can reduce the pain of stomach cramps.

Headache Ease Tea

A simple recipe to ease an upset stomach is as follows:

Ingredients:

- 1 tsp Lavender
- 1 tsp Feverfew

- 1 tsp Willow bark
- A pinch of Lemon zest

Instructions:

1. Blend lavender, feverfew, and willow bark.
2. Steep in hot water for 15 minutes. Add lemon zest.
3. Strain and enjoy.

Relieving Headaches

Headaches can strike at any moment, leaving you searching for relief. A warm cup of tea made from feverfew or willow bark, both of which have been used historically for pain relief, can offer a comforting alternative to over-the-counter options. Their natural compounds have properties that are known to reduce inflammation and ease headache pain.

Headache Ease Tea

If ever you have a headache, follow this recipe.

Ingredients:

- 1 tsp Lavender
- 1 tsp Feverfew
- 1 tsp Willow bark
- A pinch of Lemon zest

Instructions:

1. Blend lavender, feverfew, and willow bark.
2. Steep in hot water for 15 minutes. Add lemon zest.
3. Strain and enjoy.

Easing Muscle Aches

For those who experience muscle aches, whether from exertion or tension, a restorative tea blend can be a simple remedy. Ingredients such as chamomile are revered for their anti-inflammatory and relaxing properties, which can help to soothe tight muscles and reduce discomfort.

Muscle Relief Tea
This tea would help ease muscle tension. Follow the recipe below to make one yourself.

Ingredients:

- 1 tsp Valerian root
- 1 tsp Rosemary
- 1 tsp Lemon balm
- Honey *(to taste)*

Instructions:

1. Mix valerian root, rosemary, and lemon balm.
2. Steep in boiling water for 10 minutes.
3. Strain and add honey to taste.

Soothing Sore Throats

A sore throat can be the first sign of illness or a standalone irritation. Teas containing honey and lemon can provide a soothing coat to an inflamed throat, while the addition of anti-inflammatory herbs like licorice root can further calm irritation.

Throat Comfort Tea
This tea is a perfect home remedy for sore throats.

Ingredients:

- 1 tsp Licorice root
- 1 tsp Marshmallow root
- 1 small piece of Cinnamon bark
- Honey *(to taste)*

Instructions:

1. Combine licorice root, marshmallow root, and cinnamon bark in a pot with water.
2. Boil and simmer for 15 minutes.
3. Strain, add honey, and sip warm.

Boosting Energy Levels

Fatigue is a common complaint in a busy world. Instead of reaching for caffeine, a more balanced boost can be found in teas with ginseng or green tea. These herbs have energizing properties without the jitters often associated with coffee.

Energizing Herbal Blend

Feeling low in energy? This blend is for you!

Ingredients:

- 1 tsp Green tea leaves
- 1/2 tsp Ginseng
- 1 tsp Orange peel
- 1 tsp Lemongrass

Instructions:

1. Blend green tea, ginseng, orange peel, and lemongrass.
2. Steep in hot water for 5 minutes.
3. Strain and enjoy.

Calming Nervousness

In times of stress and anxiety, a cup of herbal tea can be a simple way to induce calm. Herbs like lemon balm, lavender, and valerian root are known for their calming effects on the nervous system, providing a natural way to reduce feelings of nervousness and promote relaxation.

Relaxing Nerve Tea
Feel relaxed as you sip on this tasty tea.

Ingredients:

- 1 tsp Passionflower
- 1 tsp Skullcap
- 1 tsp Lemon verbena
- Honey *(optional)*

Instructions:

1. Combine passionflower, skullcap, and lemon verbena.
2. Steep in boiling water for 10 minutes.
3. Strain and add honey if desired.

Alleviating Insomnia

If sleep eludes you, consider teas with herbs like chamomile or passionflower. These have been traditionally used to promote sleepiness and improve the quality of sleep, making them ideal for those occasional nights when you find it hard to drift off.

Sleepy Time Tea
Try making this tea if you want better sleep quality.

Ingredients:

- 1 tbsp Chamomile
- 1 tsp Lavender
- 1/2 tsp Valerian root
- 1 tsp Lemon balm

Instructions:

1. Mix chamomile, lavender, valerian root, and lemon balm.
2. Steep in hot water for 15 minutes.
3. Strain and drink before bedtime.

Recognizing the Limits of Herbal Teas

As you steep your leaves and herbs, reveling in their aroma and the promise of relief they bring, it is important to acknowledge the scope and limits of herbal remedies. While the teas mentioned are time-honored allies against daily discomforts, they are not cure-alls.

Herbal teas can provide significant relief for a variety of common symptoms, such as those from colds or temporary digestive issues. However, it is crucial to recognize that these symptoms can also be signs of more serious conditions. For instance, consistent stomach upsets could indicate a food intolerance or a gastrointestinal disorder, while frequent headaches might be a symptom of a more chronic issue.

The Importance of Medical Advice

If you find yourself reaching for the same herbal remedy time and again, it could be a signal that a deeper health issue needs addressing. Herbal teas should complement, not replace, professional medical advice and treatment. Always consider seeking guidance from a healthcare provider to explore and understand the root cause of any persistent or severe symptoms.

Safety and Efficacy

Moreover, it is important to ensure the safety and efficacy of the herbs you choose. Not all herbs are created equal, and some can interact with medications or be contraindicated in certain health conditions. It is best to do thorough research or consult with a healthcare professional, especially if you are pregnant, breastfeeding, or managing a health condition.

Informed Decisions for Better Health

Remember, your health is a narrative that intertwines various chapters of remedies, lifestyle choices, and medical insights. Herbal teas are a valuable chapter in that narrative, but they are most effective when used in conjunction with a broader understanding of your health. Make informed decisions and listen to your body; if symptoms persist, they may be whispering the need for deeper investigation and care.

Hormonal Health and Wellness

As you dive deep into hormonal health, it is important to realize that your endocrine system—the network of glands that produce hormones—affects every aspect of your health. Herbal teas can play a role in nurturing this complex system.

Importance of Hormonal Health and Balance

The importance of hormones can hardly be overstated. These potent chemicals circulate throughout your body, influencing nearly every aspect of your health. From your metabolic rate to your heart rate, growth to mood regulation, hormones are critical to your body's homeostasis or balance. Imagine them as conductors of an orchestra, ensuring that every section comes in at the right time, neither too loudly nor too softly, to create a harmonious symphony of bodily functions.

Consequences of Hormonal Imbalance

Yet, just as in an orchestra, a misstep in one section can throw off the entire performance, and a hormonal imbalance can lead to a cascade of health issues. You might, for example, find yourself feeling unusually fatigued, inexplicably gaining weight, or facing irregular menstrual cycles. These are not just random occurrences but can be indicative of hormonal disruption. Such imbalances can be particularly insidious because they often develop slowly over time, making them harder to detect and address.

Recognizing the Signals of Disruption

Your body communicates through symptoms, and recognizing these signs can be your first clue to a hormonal imbalance. Perhaps you have noticed that your skin breaks out in acne before your period, or you are struggling with sleep disturbances that leave you restless at night. These fluctuations are your body's distress signals, urging you to pay attention to deeper issues that may be at play.

It is essential to understand that while some fluctuations in hormone levels are normal — *such as those that occur during the menstrual cycle or as a part of aging* — others may indicate an underlying health condition that requires attention. Being attuned to your body's signals is the first step in addressing any imbalances.

The Power of Prevention

One of the most empowering aspects of understanding hormonal health is prevention. By identifying the lifestyle factors that contribute to hormonal imbalance, such as poor diet, insufficient sleep, excessive stress, and exposure to environmental toxins, you can take proactive steps to maintain balance. Regular exercise, a balanced diet, stress management techniques, and adequate sleep are all pivotal in supporting hormonal health.

Gender-Specific Benefits of Herbal Teas

While the endocrine system—the network responsible for hormone production and regulation—is fundamentally similar in everyone, hormonal health can vary widely between genders. Men and women have a unique hormonal blueprint, influencing everything from reproductive health to muscle mass and bone density. Recognizing this, herbal teas can be selected and formulated to support these distinctive needs.

Teas for Women's Health

Women often face hormonal fluctuations throughout their lives, such as during menstrual cycles, pregnancy, and menopause. These changes can sometimes lead to discomfort or health issues that can be soothed by specific herbal infusions.

- **Black Cohosh Tea**: A time-honored remedy for women, black cohosh can help mitigate menopausal symptoms such as hot flashes and mood swings. A simple recipe involves steeping one teaspoon of dried black cohosh root in boiling water for 20 minutes. This earthy tea can be sipped twice a day for relief.
- **Nettle Tea**: Loaded with iron and other minerals, nettle is a tonic for women's health, particularly during menstrua-

tion, to replenish lost nutrients. To enjoy nettle tea, infuse one to two teaspoons of dried nettle leaves in hot water for 10 minutes. Drink daily to harness its full spectrum of benefits.

- **Red Clover Tea:** Beneficial for hormonal balance, Red Clover is rich in isoflavones, which are plant-based chemicals that mimic estrogen. To make red clover tea, steep one teaspoon of dried red clover blossoms in a cup of boiling water for 15 minutes. It is recommended to drink one cup daily.
- **Dong Quai Tea:** Revered in traditional Chinese medicine, Dong Quai is known as a *'female ginseng.'* It is believed to balance estrogen levels and relieve menstrual symptoms. To prepare, steep one teaspoon of dried Dong Quai root in hot water for 15 minutes. Drink once daily.
- **Spearmint Tea:** Helpful in managing hormonal imbalances such as PCOS. Brew by steeping one tablespoon of fresh or dried spearmint leaves in boiling water for 5 to 10 minutes.
- **Evening Primrose Tea:** Known for its potential to alleviate premenstrual and menopausal symptoms. Steep one teaspoon of dried evening primrose flowers in boiling water for about 10 minutes.

Teas for Men's Health

While less discussed, men also experience hormonal shifts, particularly concerning testosterone levels as they age. Certain teas can help support men's hormonal health, contributing to better overall well-being.

- **Saw Palmetto Tea**: Traditionally used to support prostate health, saw palmetto can be beneficial for men, especially those looking to maintain a healthy urinary tract. To make this tea, steep about one gram of dried saw palmetto berries in hot water for 10 minutes. This can be taken daily, with meals.

- **Fenugreek Tea**: Studies suggest that fenugreek may enhance testosterone levels and improve libido. To prepare fenugreek tea, simmer one teaspoon of fenugreek seeds in water for 5 minutes. Strain and drink twice a day to potentially boost vitality.
- **Tribulus Terrestris Tea:** Known for supporting male reproductive health, Tribulus Terrestris may also aid in increasing testosterone levels. Brew by steeping one teaspoon of dried Tribulus Terrestris in a cup of boiling water for 10 minutes. Enjoy this tea once a day.
- **Green Tea with Mint:** Green tea is known for its antioxidant properties, while mint can add a refreshing taste. Combine one teaspoon of green tea leaves and a few fresh mint leaves in hot water. Steep for 3 to 5 minutes, strain, and enjoy. This tea can be consumed twice daily.

Life Stage-Specific Tea Blends

Life is a dynamic journey, with each stage presenting its own set of health challenges and needs, especially when it comes to hormonal balance. Each life stage is unique, with its rhythm and needs, and herbal teas can be a natural part of your health regimen through each one. When you choose teas that are suited to your current life phase, you are honoring your body's specific hormonal requirements. From the tumultuous years of adolescence to the reflective twilight of maturity, herbal teas can provide support tailored to these shifting requirements.

Teas for Adolescents

Adolescence is a whirlwind of change, and hormones are at the center of this transformation. Teens may benefit from herbal teas that cater to hormonal balance and stress relief.

- **Chamomile Tea**: With its gentle calming effects, chamomile can be a teenager's ally against stress and anxiety. A simple recipe involves steeping 1 to 2 teaspoons of chamomile flowers in hot water for 5-10 minutes. This tea can be enjoyed in the evening to encourage relaxation.
- **Lemon Balm Tea**: Known for improving mood and cognitive function, lemon balm can help manage the emotional ups and downs of puberty. Use 1 tablespoon of dried lemon balm per cup of boiling water, steeping for about 10 minutes.

Teas for Reproductive Years

The reproductive years bring about a renewed focus on the hormonal system, particularly for those interested in conception and maintaining regular menstrual cycles.

- **Raspberry Leaf Tea**: Celebrated for its benefits during pregnancy, raspberry leaf can also promote menstrual cycle regularity. Brew by pouring boiling water over 1 teaspoon of dried leaves, steeping for at least 5 minutes.
- **Vitex Berry Tea**: Also known as chaste tree berry, vitex is lauded for balancing hormones related to reproductive health. Prepare by steeping 1 teaspoon of dried berries in hot water for 10 minutes.
- **Maca Root Tea:** Maca root is known for its hormone-balancing and fertility-enhancing properties. Prepare by adding 1 teaspoon of maca root powder to a cup of hot water and stirring well. Consume this earthy tea daily for hormonal support.
- **Angelica Root Tea:** Known for its ability to support female reproductive health, angelica root is often used to regulate menstrual cycles. Brew the tea by steeping one.

Teas for Mature Adults

As the body ages, hormonal support shifts towards maintaining energy, cognitive function, and overall vitality.

- **Ginseng Tea**: A revered adaptogen, ginseng can help combat fatigue and support mental alertness in older adults. Simmer 1 teaspoon of ginseng root in water for 15 to 20 minutes for a stimulating brew.
- **Ginkgo Biloba Tea**: Ginkgo is often associated with enhancing memory and cognitive speed. To prepare, steep 1 teaspoon of dried ginkgo leaves in hot water for about 10 minutes.

Understanding Herb-Drug Interactions

As more individuals turn towards complementary and alternative medicine, the concurrent use of prescription drugs and herbal remedies has become increasingly common. This intersection can lead to potent interactions that may enhance or diminish the effectiveness of medications, pose serious health risks, or offer beneficial synergies.

Potential Interactions and Their Implications

The stakes are high when it comes to mixing herbs and pharmaceuticals. The compounds found in herbs can interact with drugs by affecting their metabolism, transport, and elimination from the body, potentially leading to unexpected outcomes.

For instance, the herb St. John's Wort is notorious for its ability to induce liver enzymes, which can hasten the breakdown of various drugs, including oral contraceptives, thereby diminishing their effectiveness and potentially leading to unintended pregnancies. Other herbs might amplify a drug's impact, which can be equally concerning. For example, using blood-thinning herbs like Ginkgo biloba in conjunction with anticoagulant medications can increase the risk of bleeding, a side effect that can have serious or even life-threatening consequences.

Common Herb-Drug Interactions

Navigating the landscape of herb-drug interactions requires a keen understanding of how certain herbal teas can impact the effectiveness of prescription medications. Here are more examples to consider:

- **Anticoagulants and Ginger**: Ginger has natural blood-thinning properties, which can intensify the effects of anticoagulant drugs such as heparin or warfarin, increasing the risk of bleeding.
- **Diuretics and Licorice Root**: Licorice root can decrease potassium levels in the body. When taken with diuretics, which also lower potassium, it may lead to a significant drop, causing muscle weakness or abnormal heart rhythms.
- **Blood Pressure Medications and Hawthorn**: Hawthorn is often used for heart health but can enhance the effects of some blood pressure medications, potentially causing blood pressure to drop too low.
- **Thyroid Medications and Soy**: Soy, found in some herbal preparations, can interfere with the body's ability to absorb thyroid medication, necessitating adjustments in dosing.
- **Antidiabetic Drugs and Cinnamon**: While cinnamon is touted for its ability to lower blood sugar, it can cause an additive effect when taken with antidiabetic drugs, leading to hypoglycemia *(low blood sugar levels)*.
- **Sedatives and Valerian Root**: Valerian root is commonly used for its sedative properties. If taken with prescription

sedatives, it can compound their effects, potentially resulting in excessive sedation or respiratory depression.

- **Immune Suppressants and Echinacea**: Echinacea is known for boosting the immune system. For those on immune suppressants, this could counteract the effects of their medication, potentially reducing its efficacy.
- **Oral Contraceptives and St. John's Wort**: Beyond St. John's Wort's effect on depression medications, it can also accelerate the breakdown of hormones in birth control, reducing its contraceptive effects.
- **Antibiotics and Tannins**: Tannins, present in teas like black tea and certain herbal teas, can inhibit the absorption of certain antibiotics, making them less effective.
- **Calcium Channel Blockers and Grapefruit**: While not an herb, grapefruit *(including herbal preparations containing grapefruit extract)* deserves mention for its significant interaction with various medications, including some calcium channel blockers used for heart conditions, by increasing their levels in the blood.

Longevity Teas

Herbal teas are not just about addressing immediate symptoms—they can also be about nurturing your long-term health. One key to promoting longevity is to combat oxidative stress—the same process that causes metals to rust and apples to brown.

Herbal Teas for Detoxification

Your body is naturally equipped with detoxification systems, and some herbal teas can support this crucial function.

- **Milk Thistle Tea**: Milk thistle is celebrated for its silymarin content, which can help rejuvenate liver cells and protect against harmful toxins.

- **Dandelion Tea**: Often considered just a weed, dandelion is a potent detoxifier, especially for the liver, and aids in digestion.
- **Burdock Root Tea:** Known for its blood-purifying properties, burdock root supports liver function and skin health. To brew, add one tablespoon of dried burdock root to boiling water. Simmer for 10 minutes, strain, and drink once a day.
- **Green Tea with Lemon:** Green tea is rich in antioxidants, and when combined with lemon, it enhances the detoxifying effects. Brew one teaspoon of green tea leaves in hot water for 3 to 5 minutes, add a slice of lemon, and enjoy this refreshing and cleansing tea.
- **Ginger and Turmeric Tea:** Both ginger and turmeric are known for their detoxifying and anti-inflammatory properties. Steep a 1-inch piece of fresh ginger and a teaspoon of turmeric in boiling water for 10 minutes. Strain and sip to aid digestion and liver function.

Nurturing Cognitive Function with Herbal Teas

Maintaining brain health is a pillar of longevity. Certain herbs can help support cognitive function and potentially ward off the fog of aging.

- **Ginkgo Biloba Tea**: Ginkgo has long been used to improve memory and reduce mental fatigue. Steep dried ginkgo leaves for a tea that supports brain health.
- **Gotu Kola Tea**: Revered in Ayurvedic medicine, gotu kola can help improve circulation and cognitive function. A simple tea can be made from its leaves for daily consumption.

Heart Health and Herbal Teas

The heart is central to life, and herbal teas can be a soothing way to support cardiac function.

- **Hibiscus Tea**: With its tart flavor, hibiscus has been shown to help lower high blood pressure, a major risk factor for heart disease.
- **Garlic Tea**: Though not a traditional tea ingredient, garlic can be infused in hot water and mixed with honey to create a potent drink that helps manage cholesterol levels.

Recipes for Long-Term Health Teas

To craft these teas, you do not need to be an herbalist—just a curious mind and a love for natural wellness. Here are a couple of recipes to get you started:

Daily Antioxidant Boost Tea

- 1 teaspoon of dried green tea leaves
- 1 teaspoon of rooibos
- Honey to taste
- Lemon wedge for an extra vitamin C kick

Steep the green tea and rooibos in boiling water for 5 minutes. Strain, add honey and lemon to taste, and enjoy once daily.

Cognitive Clarity Tea

- 1 teaspoon of dried ginkgo biloba leaves
- 1 teaspoon of gotu kola leaves
- A slice of fresh ginger for added zest and benefits

Infuse the ginkgo biloba, gotu kola, and ginger in hot water for 10 minutes. Strain and sip mindfully, ideally in the morning or early afternoon.

Inflammation and Pain Management

Explore how herbal teas can be specifically tailored to combat inflammation and manage pain—a duo of discomfort that plagues many.

Understanding Inflammation's Impact

On the one hand, acute inflammation is the body's innate defense mechanism, a beneficial response that signals our immune system to heal an injury or fight an infection. On the other, chronic inflammation is a stealthy adversary that can undermine our health if left unchecked.

When inflammation persists or serves no purpose, it can create a chronic, low-grade inflammatory response throughout the body, triggering cellular damage and contributing to the development of various diseases. This chronic inflammation can be likened to a persistent alarm that fails to switch off, leading to a cascade of biological disruptions. It is this type of inflammation that is often the focus when we talk about inflammation-related diseases.

In the context of pain management, chronic inflammation is particularly significant because it is a common cause of long-lasting pain. This pain is not just a symptom; it can also contribute to the perpetuation of inflammation, creating a vicious cycle that can be difficult to break.

Why Target Inflammation?

Inflammation is a double-edged sword: it is the body's essential response to injury or infection, yet when it becomes chronic, it can silently underpin a host of diseases and affect overall well-being.

- **Prevention of Chronic Diseases**: By managing inflammation, you can help prevent the onset of many chronic diseases. Studies have shown that chronic inflammation can lead to the development of certain cancers, heart disease, and Alzheimer's disease.
- **Improved Longevity**: Reducing inflammation can not only improve quality of life but also extend it. Inflammation is one of the contributing factors to the aging process. By curbing inflammation, you are supporting your body in maintaining its functions for a longer period.
- **Enhanced Daily Functioning**: Even day-to-day well-being is affected by inflammation. It can cause fatigue, pain, and mood swings. By keeping inflammation in check, you can improve your daily energy levels, mood, and overall sense of well-being.
- **Support for Mental Health**: Emerging research suggests that inflammation may also play a role in mental health conditions such as depression and anxiety. Addressing inflammation could be part of a comprehensive approach to mental health care.

The Role of Herbal Teas in Combating Inflammation

Inflammation and pain are two of the body's most fundamental responses to injury or disease, and they often go hand in hand. Managing these symptoms is a cornerstone of medical treatment, yet many patients are turning to herbal remedies as adjuncts or alternatives to pharmaceuticals. Herbal teas, in particular, offer a soothing and natural means of easing discomfort.

The curative potential of herbal teas lies in their bioactive constituents, which can possess anti-inflammatory and analgesic properties. For example, ginger tea, with its potent gingerol compound, can inhibit inflammatory pathways in the body, thereby reducing swelling and pain. Similarly, turmeric tea, rich in curcumin, has been shown to alleviate chronic inflammation, which is at the heart of many pain-related conditions.

Moreover, the ritual of preparing and sipping tea can itself be a meditative and restorative process, offering psychological comfort that may enhance the physical benefits. By incorporating these practices into a comprehensive pain management plan, individuals may find additional relief and a greater sense of well-being.

Fighting Against Inflammation

Chronic inflammation often flies under the radar, quietly contributing to a host of health issues from arthritis to heart disease. It is a stealthy adversary but not an invincible one. A proactive approach includes integrating anti-inflammatory herbal teas into your diet.

Turmeric

Turmeric, with its active component curcumin, is a celebrated anti-inflammatory herb. When you incorporate turmeric tea into your routine, you are enlisting a powerful ally in the fight against inflammation.

Turmeric Tea Recipe:

- 1 teaspoon of ground turmeric or a 1-inch piece of fresh turmeric root, sliced
- A pinch of black pepper *(to enhance curcumin absorption)*

- 1 teaspoon of honey or maple syrup for sweetness
- A slice of lemon or a dash of lemon juice for a vitamin C boost

Simmer the turmeric and black pepper in 2 cups of water for 10 minutes. Strain into a mug, stir in sweetener, and add lemon to taste.

Ginger

Ginger, with its zesty flavor, is not just a spice for your food; it is also a powerful anti-inflammatory herb. Regularly sipping on ginger tea can help reduce inflammation and alleviate associated pains like those from osteoarthritis.

Ginger Tea Recipe:

- A 2-inch piece of fresh ginger root, thinly sliced
- Honey or another natural sweetener to taste
- **Optional:** Add a cinnamon stick for additional anti-inflammatory benefits

Boil the ginger slices in 2 cups of water for 20 minutes to fully extract the flavors. Remove from heat, strain, add sweetener, and enjoy. For an extra flavor dimension, include a cinnamon stick while boiling.

Chamomile

Chamomile is often praised for its calming effects, but it is also a subtle warrior against inflammation, particularly helpful in soothing the digestive system.

Chamomile Tea Recipe:

- 1 tablespoon of dried chamomile flowers or 1 chamomile tea bag
- Boiling water
- Optional: A sprig of mint or a slice of fresh ginger for additional benefits

Pour boiling water over chamomile flowers and allow to steep for 5 minutes. If using, add mint or ginger before steeping for an extra soothing effect. Strain and serve.

CHAPTER 9

Fitness and Energy Teas

This chapter explores how teas can enhance fitness and naturally increase endurance. You will discover how teas can provide an invigorating caffeine-free alternative with ingredients that optimize energy, metabolism, and workout recovery. Adaptogenic teas are highlighted for their stress-relieving and performance-enhancing properties. From metabolism-boosting brews to pre-workout pep, these tips will help you create an energizing tea routine.

Vitality-Boosting Teas

In the relentless rhythm of contemporary life, you may often seek that extra surge of energy to power through the day. Vitality-boosting teas could be your solution—a natural, calming cup that awakens your senses and lifts your spirit without the harsh buzz of caffeine.

Teas as Caffeine Alternatives

When it comes to stimulating your senses and giving you that much-needed boost, caffeine is often the go-to. However, it is not uncommon to hear about the less desirable effects of caffeine, such as restlessness, insomnia, and a dreaded crash. This is where the world of teas offers a soothing sanctuary. They are the natural allies in your quest for a gentle lift without the unwanted side effects.

Teas naturally contain a variety of compounds that can have stimulating effects on the body, but they often do so more gently than caffeine. For example, teas generally have a lower caffeine content, which means they can provide an energy boost without the intense rush and subsequent crash.

Many teas, especially green tea, contain L-theanine, an amino acid that promotes relaxation without drowsiness. This compound works synergistically with the small amounts of caffeine present in tea to produce a state of mindful alertness. It smooths out the energy boost, mitigating the highs and lows associated with coffee, and helps maintain a focused calm.

Teas are also rich in antioxidants, such as catechins and polyphenols. These substances do more than just fight off cellular damage—they can also contribute to a sense of increased energy. Antioxidants help optimize the body's processes, which can lead to a natural and healthy feeling of vigor.

Uplifting Tea Recipes

Unlike the sharp jolt delivered by a cup of coffee, the energy from tea feels more balanced. It is like waking naturally with the sunrise rather than being jolted awake by an alarm. This smoother curve of energy provided by tea is conducive to sustained focus and productivity, making it an ideal beverage for both relaxation and tasks that require prolonged attention. Whether you are looking for a substitute for your morning coffee or an afternoon pick-me-up, the following tea recipes offer a delicious and healthy way to boost your vitality.

Yerba Mate Marvel

Yerba mate is renowned for its balanced, energizing effects and is a staple in South American cultures. It contains mateine, a compound similar to caffeine, without the typical side effects.

1. Steep 1 tablespoon of yerba mate leaves in hot water for 3 to 5 minutes.
2. Strain the leaves and add a slice of lemon or a dash of honey for a flavorful twist.

Ginseng Vitality Brew

Ginseng tea is a revered herbal tea known for its energy-boosting properties.

- Steep ginseng root slices or ginseng tea bag in boiling water for 5 to 10 minutes.
- Enhance with a bit of honey and a sprinkle of cinnamon to taste.

Guayusa Leaf Glow

Guayusa is another herbal tea that naturally contains caffeine and is often used as a coffee alternative for sustained energy.

1. Brew guayusa leaves in hot water for about 5 minutes.
2. Add a slice of green apple and a stick of lemongrass as it steeps for a refreshing twist.

Green Tea Zest

Green tea is famous for its subtle caffeine content and high antioxidant levels, making it a perfect choice for a gentle energy lift.

1. Steep 1 teaspoon of green tea leaves in hot water for 2 to 3 minutes.
2. Add a twist of lemon zest and a teaspoon of honey for a refreshing and energizing cup.

Matcha Mint Infusion

Matcha, a powdered form of green tea, provides a unique blend of calm energy and alertness thanks to its combination of caffeine and L-theanine.

1. Whisk 1 teaspoon of matcha powder in hot water until frothy.
2. Add a few fresh mint leaves for a cool, invigorating flavor.

Hibiscus and Berry Boost

Hibiscus tea, with its tart flavor, pairs well with berries for a refreshing and uplifting drink.

1. Steep dried hibiscus flowers and a handful of mixed berries in boiling water for 5 minutes.
2. Strain and sweeten with honey or agave nectar if desired.

Rooibos & Orange Revival

Rooibos is a naturally caffeine-free tea that can be a great afternoon pick-me-up, especially when combined with citrus flavors.

1. Steep 1 tablespoon of rooibos tea leaves with a few slices of fresh orange in hot water for 5 to 7 minutes.
2. Sweeten with a bit of honey and garnish with an orange slice.

Workout Energizers

The teas you choose can make all the difference. Pre-workout, savor a cup of herbal tea to gently awaken and prepare your body for exercise. Post-exercise, opt for a blend that supports recovery and rehydration.

Pre-Workout Teas

As you gear up for an invigorating workout, your choice of fuel is crucial. Pre-workout teas are a go-to for many fitness enthusiasts, not just for the caffeine boost but for the natural synergy of compounds that prime your body for exertion.

Mint

If you prefer a cooler sensation, mint tea can be invigorating. The natural menthol in mint leaves sparks a refreshing feeling that can enhance your breathing as you exercise. It is like taking a deep breath of cool morning air and setting a brisk tempo for your workout.

Post-Workout Recovery with Tea

After pushing your limits and sweating it out, your body enters a crucial phase of recovery. It is a time when the right nutrients and hydration can make all the difference in how quickly and effectively your body heals and strengthens.

Chamomile

Chamomile tea is often associated with sleep and relaxation, but its benefits extend into the realm of physical recovery. It contains natural properties that can help soothe muscle spasms and reduce inflammation. Imagine sipping on a warm cup of chamomile tea, feeling each muscle relax as the herb's gentle effects take hold, easing the tension and tightness from your workout.

Turmeric

Turmeric tea, with its vibrant golden hue, offers a wealth of recovery benefits. The active compound, curcumin, is a powerhouse of anti-inflammatory properties, helping to alleviate the soreness and inflammation that often follow a strenuous workout. However, curcumin is not easily absorbed on its own. This is where a pinch of black pepper comes into play, containing piperine, a compound that enhances the absorption of curcumin by up to 2000%. It is not just about mixing ingredients; it is about unlocking their potential.

Peppermint

Peppermint tea is another excellent choice for post-workout recovery. Its cooling properties can provide a refreshing sensation, which can be particularly welcome after a sweat-inducing exercise session. Additionally, peppermint has natural muscle-relaxant properties that may help reduce stiffness.

Electrolytes and Herbal Teas

Electrolytes are like the body's spark plugs, essential for the electrical wiring that keeps everything running smoothly. These charged particles regulate nerve and muscle function, hydrate the body, balance blood acidity and pressure, and help rebuild damaged tissue. After a workout, your electrolyte levels can be significantly depleted, which is why replenishing them is crucial.

Herbal Solutions for Electrolyte Replenishment

In seeking equilibrium, herbal teas emerge as a natural ally. They offer a dual benefit: hydration and the replenishment of essential minerals. Here are some herbal teas for this.

Hibiscus Tea

Hibiscus tea is a brilliant red infusion known for its tart flavor and vitamin C content. But beyond its tangy taste, hibiscus is a treasure trove of minerals like potassium and magnesium, which are vital components of the electrolyte family. Drinking hibiscus tea can help restore the electrolytes lost through sweat during a workout.

Coconut Water Tea

When you think of electrolytes, coconut water might be one of the first things that come to mind. It is nature's sports drink, rich in electrolytes like sodium, potassium, and magnesium. But have you ever considered coconut water tea? By steeping delicate teas in coconut water or adding coconut water to a brewed tea, you create a hydrating powerhouse. This coconut water tea fusion provides a tropical twist that is not only hydrating but also replenishing, perfect for post-workout recovery.

Peppermint and Cucumber Hydration Tisane

A cooling and refreshing option, this tisane blends the soothing properties of peppermint with the hydrating benefits of cucumber. Cucumbers are a great source of potassium, adding essential minerals to this drink. The combination is perfect for rehydration and revitalizing the body, especially after physical activities or during hot weather.

Teas for Weight Management

Embarking on a journey of weight loss often involves navigating through a maze of dietary advice and fitness regimens. Amidst this complex pursuit, teas emerge as a simple yet potent ally.

The Role of Teas in Weight Loss

When you are tackling weight management, the principle is straightforward: the energy you consume through food should be balanced by the energy you expend through daily activities and exercise. Teas, especially certain varieties, can nudge this balance in your favor.

Dive into your pantry, and you might find a treasure trove of weight management in the form of tea leaves. Many herbal teas—such as peppermint, hibiscus, and rooibos—may support weight loss efforts. They do not contain caffeine like green tea, but they can still play a role in managing weight through different mechanisms.

For instance, certain herbal teas may promote a feeling of fullness, reducing the likelihood of overeating. Others might aid digestion or metabolism without the added effect of caffeine-induced thermogenesis. They are also practically calorie-free, which means you can enjoy a satisfying cup without affecting your daily caloric limit—so long as you forego any sweeteners. Moreover, the rich and diverse flavors of herbal teas can act as a palate cleanser, diminishing the urge for sugary snacks.

Metabolism-Boosting Herbal Selections

Think of your metabolism as a furnace within your body, consuming fuel at a rate that can determine how efficiently you lose weight. The right herbs found in teas can serve as a catalyst, turning up the heat on your metabolism. These have unique properties that can assist in accelerating the body's metabolic processes. Here, you will discover a selection of herbal teas celebrated for their metabolism-enhancing properties.

Dandelion Root Tea

Dandelion root is often associated with detoxification. It supports digestion and may help to balance the digestive tract, facilitating a more efficient metabolic process.

Ingredients:

- 1 tbsp roasted dandelion root
- 1/2 tsp cinnamon powder
- 1 tsp honey
- 2 cups water

Instructions:

1. In a saucepan, bring water to a boil.
2. Add roasted dandelion root and cinnamon powder.
3. Simmer for 10 minutes.
4. Strain into a cup and stir in honey.
5. Enjoy this earthy and slightly spicy tea.

Cinnamon Tea

Cinnamon is a warming spice that has been shown to help regulate blood sugar levels, which can help manage cravings and maintain even energy levels throughout the day.

Ingredients:

- 1 cinnamon stick
- 1/2 tsp ground turmeric
- 1/4 tsp black pepper
- 1 tsp honey
- 2 cups water

Instructions:

1. Boil water with the cinnamon stick for 10 minutes.
2. Add turmeric and black pepper and simmer for an additional 5 minutes.
3. Strain into a mug and sweeten with honey.
4. Sip this warmly spiced tea to help regulate blood sugar levels.

Fennel Tea

Fennel has a licorice-like taste and is traditionally used to promote digestion and prevent bloating, aiding in smoother digestion and potentially improving metabolic function.

Ingredients:

- 1 tbsp fennel seeds, crushed
- 1/2 tsp ginger, freshly grated
- 1 tsp lemon juice
- 1 tsp honey
- 2 cups water

Instructions:

1. Boil water and add crushed fennel seeds and grated ginger.
2. Simmer for 5 to 7 minutes.
3. Strain into a cup, add lemon juice and honey.
4. Enjoy this soothing tea to aid digestion and prevent bloating.

Tea Routines for Weight Goals

When you are aiming for weight loss, the structure of your daily routine can have a significant impact. Integrating tea into your daily regimen can offer a comforting rhythm while providing the added benefit of supporting your weight management efforts.

Establishing a Tea Routine

Building a tea routine is not just about enjoying a warm cup; it is about setting up a framework for success in your weight goals. It is creating a habit that not only aligns with your weight management strategy but also enhances it.

Kickstart Your Metabolism in the Morning

Begin your day with a cup of green tea. The caffeine and catechins can help to increase your metabolic rate and provide a subtle energy boost without the spike and crash associated with coffee. Try drinking it before your breakfast for an early morning metabolic kick.

Mid-Morning and Afternoon Tea Breaks

Mid-morning, reach for a cup of white tea. Its high antioxidant levels can help to keep your metabolism humming along while also providing a palate cleanser to prevent snack cravings. In the afternoon, a cup of oolong tea can serve as a bridge between meals, satisfying with its distinctive taste and keeping your metabolism active.

Control Your Appetite

Incorporate appetite-suppressing teas like peppermint or ginger tea before meals. The strong flavors can help to curb your appetite, making it easier to avoid overeating. Ginger tea, in particular, is beneficial before lunch or dinner as it can also aid digestion.

Evening Wind Down

As the day closes, a caffeine-free herbal tea like chamomile or rooibos can help to relax your body and mind. Not only does this support a healthy sleep cycle, which is crucial for weight management, but it also helps to stave off late-night cravings.

Tips for Success

By following these guidelines, you can create a tea routine that not only fits seamlessly into your day but also actively supports your journey toward reaching and maintaining your weight goals. Remember, the key to success is consistency, and a daily tea ritual can be a pleasurable and effective part of your weight management toolkit. Furthermore, use these tips so this can be more effective.

- **Stay Hydrated**: Drink a cup of herbal tea in between meals to stay hydrated and keep hunger at bay.
- **Mindful Brewing**: Use the time it takes to brew your tea to take a few deep breaths and center yourself, making your tea routine a mindful practice.
- **Avoid Additives**: Skip the sugar and cream to keep your tea's calorie count low; if you need a sweetener, opt for a small amount of honey or stevia.
- **Tea Before Treats**: If you are craving something sweet, try a cup of naturally sweet herbal tea first to satisfy the craving without the calories.

Endurance and Adaptogens

Wanting increased endurance is not just for athletes; it is a universal desire shared by anyone looking to improve their physical and mental performance in all areas of life.

Defining Adaptogens

Imagine your body is like a high-tech car. Just as this car adapts to changing terrains and conditions for a smooth ride, adaptogens help your body adjust to various stressors for optimal performance. They are the unsung heroes in the wellness world, helping you to *"adapt"* to emotional and physical stress and ensuring that your internal systems remain balanced.

Adaptogens have a unique capacity to decrease cellular sensitivity to stress. They act on the adrenal system, the part of the body responsible for managing stress, by fine-tuning your hormonal reactions. This means when you are facing a stressor—whether it is a hard workout or a challenging day at work—adaptogens work to normalize your physiological functions.

This normalization does not push your body to react more strongly or weakly to stress. Instead, adaptogens balance your response in a way that is appropriate to the situation. So, you might find that you are less jittery before a big presentation or more energized during the long run, thanks to the stabilizing effects of these natural substances.

Their impact on endurance and vitality can be profound. By supporting adrenal function and helping to regulate stress hormones like cortisol, adaptogens allow for improved focus, increased stamina, and a greater capacity for physical activity. They are not a one-size-fits-all solution; rather, they tailor their effects to your body's specific needs, promoting a state of equilibrium that can help you perform at your best, no matter what challenges come your way.

Adaptogenic Teas

Incorporating adaptogenic teas into your routine is like unlocking an ancient secret for modern vitality and endurance. These teas, steeped with the power of adaptogenic herbs, have been a cornerstone in traditional medicine for their restorative properties. Below, you will explore how to craft these powerful brews at home.

These recipes are a starting point for integrating adaptogenic teas into your life. Feel free to experiment with quantities and combinations to suit your taste and desired effects. Remember, the key to benefiting from adaptogens is regular and sustained use, so find your favorites and make them a part of your daily rituals for enduring vitality and wellness.

Rhodiola Rosea

Rhodiola's earthy flavor is perfect before physical activity or when you need mental clarity:

1. Heat water to a boil and let it sit for a minute to reduce the temperature slightly.
2. Add about a gram of dried Rhodiola Rosea root to a tea infuser.
3. Infuse in hot water for 15 to 20 minutes; this longer brewing time allows full extraction of the adaptogenic compounds.
4. Remove the infuser, pour the tea into your favorite mug, and perhaps add a slice of lemon for an extra zest.

Ashwagandha

Ashwagandha can help soothe nerves and ensure a restful sleep with this simple recipe:

1. Bring a cup of milk *(dairy or plant-based)* to a simmer.
2. Stir in a teaspoon of ashwagandha powder and a dash of cinnamon.
3. Simmer for another 10 minutes, stirring occasionally.
4. Strain into a mug and add a touch of honey for sweetness if needed.
5. Drink this in the evening to unwind after a long day.

Holy Basil

Holy Basil, or Tulsi, can be a daily stress relief with its rich, clove-like flavor:

1. Boil water and place a handful of Tulsi leaves *(or 1 to 2 teaspoons of dried Tulsi)* in a teapot.
2. Pour the hot water over the leaves and steep for about 5 minutes.
3. Strain into a cup, breathing in the aromatic steam before taking a sip.

Enjoy this tea in the late afternoon or early evening to transition from the day's stress to evening relaxation.

Licorice Root

Licorice root is naturally sweet and can be an after-meal treat to aid digestion:

1. Add a piece of dried licorice root to a cup of boiling water.
2. Let it steep for about 5 minutes for a strong, sweet flavor.
3. Remove the root and enjoy the tea after your meal to help digestion and boost energy.

Cordyceps

While not a traditional tea, Cordyceps can be brewed to support energy levels:

1. Simmer a teaspoon of Cordyceps powder in water for 10 minutes.
2. Strain the liquid and let it cool down slightly before drinking.

3. **Optional:** Mix with other teas like green tea for added flavor and benefits.

This is ideal for consumption before exercise or when an extra energy boost is needed.

Conclusion

Throughout this book, you have rediscovered your connection with the natural world, one cup of tea at a time. You have delved into history, understanding our deep-rooted relationship with these plants, and learned how to integrate their ancient wisdom into your daily routine.

From exploring herbal knowledge to practical tips for creating your tea garden, you journeyed through various topics. Insights on tea brewing, herb selection, and the joy of crafting your own blends have been shared. How each herb can support your well-being, serving as a gentle yet potent ally against modern life's stresses, was also discussed.

Above all, you understand that herbal teas are more than just a beverage—they are a daily ritual, a moment of calm, a wellness practice, and a link to nature. They remind us that sometimes, the most effective wellness strategies are the simplest.

As you close this book, may each cup you brew be a tribute to your health, and may the peace and balance you discover extend far beyond these pages, enriching every part of your life.

References

Chakraborty, R., & Sen, S. (2019). *Herbal medicine in India: Indigenous knowledge, practice, innovation and its value.* Springer Nature.

Farr, S. (2016). *Healing herbal teas: Learn to blend 101 specially formulated teas for stress management, common ailments, seasonal health, and immune support.* Storey Publishing, LLC.

Fenkl, E. A., & Purnell, L. D. (2020). *Textbook for transcultural health care: A population approach.* Springer Nature.

Green, J. (2000). *The herbal medicine-maker's handbook: A home manual.* Clarkson Potter/Ten Speed.

Herbert, V. (1995). *Total nutrition.* Macmillan.

Holmes, K., & Perlman, S. (2007). *The nidoviruses: Toward control of SARS and other nidovirus diseases.* Springer Science & Business Media.

Knaul, F. M. (2012). *Closing the cancer divide: An equity imperative.* Harvard University Press.

Rakel, B., & Mackenzie, E. R. (2006). *Complementary and alternative medicine for older adults: A guide to holistic approaches to healthy aging.* Springer Publishing Company.

St. Paul, D. J. (2020). *Types of herbal tea: Exotic herbal tea from around the world and their health benefits, uses, flavors and tea recipes.* Sylph Publishing.

Stankovic, M. S. (2020). *Medicinal plants and natural product research.* MDPI.

Straub-Bruce, L. A., & Alexander, L. M. (2014). *Dental herbalism: Natural therapies for the mouth.* Simon and Schuster.

Wachtel-Galor, S., & Benzie, I. F. F. (2011). *Herbal medicine: Biomolecular and clinical aspects, second edition.* CRC Press.

Wardle, J., & Sarris, J. (2019). *Clinical naturopathy: An evidence-based guide to practice.* Elsevier Health Sciences.

Exclusive Bonuses

Dear Reader,

It's with great pleasure that I present to you an exquisite collection of bonuses, carefully curated to enrich your exploration into the world of herbal teas and aromatherapy. These bonuses are designed to deepen your understanding, expand your knowledge, and enhance your experience as you journey through the realms of natural wellness and sensory delights.

- **Bonus 1 - Whispers in the Cup: A Beginner's Guide to Tasseography**
  Dive into the mystical world of tea leaf reading with this comprehensive guide. Discover the ancient art of tasseography and learn how to interpret the symbols and patterns formed by tea leaves in your cup. This bonus will introduce you to the basics, offer step-by-step instructions, and provide insights to unlock the secrets held within the whispers of your tea.

- **Bonus 2 - Scents and Serenity: Blending Herbal Tea and Aromatherapy for Wellness**
  Experience the harmonious blend of herbal tea and aromatherapy. This bonus explores how the aromatic properties of herbs can enhance the therapeutic benefits of your tea, creating a holistic approach to wellness. Learn about essential oils, their compatibility with different teas,

and how to create the perfect ambiance for relaxation and rejuvenation.

- **Bonus 3 - Historical Figures and Their Favorite Teas**
  Embark on a fascinating journey through history with this intriguing bonus. Discover the favorite teas of renowned historical figures and the stories behind their preferences. From royalty to literary giants, uncover how tea influenced their lives, inspired their work, and became a part of their legacy.

- **Bonus 4 - Herbal Tea and Festivals: A Global Celebration**
  Explore the rich cultural tapestry of herbal tea traditions around the world. This bonus takes you on a global tour of festivals and celebrations where herbal tea plays a central role. Learn about the significance of tea in various cultures, traditional brewing methods, and how tea is used in ceremonial practices and festive occasions.

- **Bonus 5 - Transformative Journeys: Embracing Natural Health**
  This bonus invites you to embrace a holistic approach to health and wellness. Discover the transformative power of incorporating herbal teas and natural remedies into your daily routine. Learn about the healing properties of different herbs, how to create your own wellness tea blends, and tips for living a more natural, balanced life.

How to Access Your Bonuses:
Scan the QR Code Below: Simply use your phone's camera or a QR code reader to scan the code, and you will be directed straight to the bonus content.

Embark on this captivating journey, and let these bonuses be your guide to a world where tradition meets tranquility, and every sip is a step towards wellness.

Warmest regards,

Astrid Brown

Made in United States
Troutdale, OR
12/07/2025

43224258R00106